The Basilica of Saint Mary

VOICES FROM A LANDMARK

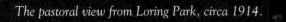

The pastoral view from Loring Park, circa 1914.

The Basilica of Saint Mary

VOICES FROM A LANDMARK

BY PEG GUILFOYLE

The Basilica of Saint Mary
Voices from a Landmark

Basilica of Saint Mary
88 North 17th Street
Minneapolis, MN 55403

Designer: Evans McCormick Creative
Copy Editor: Ann Schroeder

For information or to place an order for this book, contact:
Basilica of Saint Mary
P.O. Box 50010
Minneapolis, MN 55405-0010

Phone: 612-333-6023
Fax: 612-371-9776

e-mail: basilicahistory@mary.org

ISBN: 0-9701724-0-0

On the cover: On June 6, 1929, two thousand pupils of the sixth, seventh, and
eighth grades of the Catholic parochial schools of Minneapolis assembled on
the steps of the Basilica after a pontifical high Mass. The children sang the
Mass under the direction of the Reverend Francis Missia of St. Paul Seminary,
director of the Basilica choir. John J. Beck presided at the organ.

The Basilica of Saint Mary wishes to thank

Dr. and Mrs. Michael Paparella

*whose generous support made
this book possible.*

ACKNOWLEDGMENTS

A work like this, which draws on the memories of so many people, also has many people to thank. Dozens of parishioners sent in photos, e-mails, notes, yellowed newspaper clippings, and tattered manila envelopes with bits of Basilica history. Only a portion of that material is represented here, but all of it is now in the Basilica archives. Many people gave generously of their time in personal and phone interviews with me, and their stories make up the lively core of the book.

The Basilica's volunteer research committee provided me with the first bulging binder of materials, responded to my endless inquiries, and drew up the list of people to be interviewed. A volunteer fact-checking committee pored over the manuscript draft; thanks to Margaret Majewski, Kaylynn Wrobel, Mary Harvey, Mary Quinn Kelly, Melissa Streit, and Janet Hughes.

Overseeing all these volunteers was the indomitable Diana Gulden, who started the project without any idea that it would be so much work, and then kept going anyway.

Our volunteer researchers called regularly on local history collections. Thanks to Todd Mahon at the Hennepin History Museum, Patrick Anzelc and Steve Granger at the Archdiocese of St. Paul and Minneapolis archives, LaVette Rainer at the *Minneapolis Star Tribune*, John Walton at the *Catholic Spirit*, staff at the Minnesota Historical Society and at the Special Collections department of the Minneapolis Public Library. Early help was provided by Deborah Morse-Kahn. Thanks also to Marion Hartz.

The book draws freely on articles and photos from the *Basilica Magazine*, produced entirely by volunteers. Photographer Michael Jensen shot photos of people and objects, enriching the historical photos with beautiful slices of the present. Rita Nagan helped in the archives of the Basilica and then again with production. Keith McCormick's design and wise input has shaped the final product. Ann Schroeder's vigilant copyediting made it all sound better.

Readers for the Basilica were Father Michael O'Connell, Johan van Parys, and Terri Ashmore. Basilica staff members and parish leaders helped track down answers to a thousand research questions. Thanks also to Patricia Hampl for her reading and comments.

Many thanks to Dr. Michael and Treva Paparella for their love of history and their ongoing support of Basilica projects. As interested members of the Minneapolis community, their generous financial support made the book project possible, and allowed the proceeds from book sales to support ongoing restoration of the Basilica of Saint Mary. More than fifty others donated to the support of this book project.

This book was drawn together in a very short period of time, and I am grateful for the patience of my family, whose business occasionally went untended while I pored over stacks of photos, e-mails, faxes, and research materials. Thank you Doc, John, and Margaret. Also to my mother Joan Guilfoyle and aunt Jane Condon, whose lifelong association with their parish churches has deepened my understanding of community. My own church community does the same.

There is a great deal of history here. Inevitably, there is also a great deal not represented. There are many more conversations to come. The Basilica of Saint Mary archives invites more contributions of photos, stories, and memories.

As a writer who is not an historian, not an archivist, not even a member of the Basilica community, I fell in love with the Basilica church and with its people, both past and present. Again, thanks.

—Peg Guilfoyle
March 2000

The Basilica of Saint Mary is grateful to the following for their generous support of this book.

Winston and Barbara Adams
Mrs. Susan Arzt
Dr. Emmanuel and Mrs. Ophelia Balcos
Raymond and Mary Lou Barton
Michael and Patricia Brennan
Darlene J. and Richard P. Carroll
Thomas and Martha Casey
Joseph P. Cavaleri
Ann and Michael V. Ciresi
Gerald and Dolores Commers
Eileen D. Cooke
Lawrence and Virginia Coss
    The Coss Foundation
Ms. Patricia Miles and Mr. David Cowley
Meredyth Anne Dasburg Foundation
Wm. C. Dietrich
Mike and Kathy Dougherty
Eunice L. Dwan
Mary and Melinda Falk
    In Memory of Michael Falk
Archbishop Harry J. Flynn
Dr. and Mrs. Fredrick C. Goetz
Dennis and Jane Grendahl
Joan and Michael C. Gresser
Pierson and Florence Grieve
John and Beverly Grundhofer
Jose Peris and Diana Gulden
John and Karleen Hagan
Jim and Donna Howard
Thomas D. Jardine

Todd and Jennifer Johnson
James R. and M. Joann Jundt
Bill and Pat Kleinman
Kyle E. Kossol and Thomas M. Becker
Mary Elizabeth Lahiff
Phyllis and Standford Lehmberg
LeRoy and Colleen E. Lilly
Patrick J. Mahon
McGough Companies
Peggy and Phil McLaughlin
Mark R. Migliori
Dr. and Mrs. Daniel Moos
Franchelle and James Mullin Family
Dr. Glen Nelson and Marilyn Carlson Nelson
Dr. and Mrs. Frederick W. Noble
Irene A. Ostrowski
John A. and Agnes D. Palys
Carl and Eloise Pohlad
Joanne Provo
Archbishop John R. Roach
Raphael P. Schlingerman
Timothy D. Sellner and Ann-Marie Foerst
Mr. and Mrs. Michael E. Shannon
Kerry L. Sheehy, M.D.
Louis and Mary Kay Smith
Maurice and Estelle Spiegel
Brenda Wehle and John Carroll Lynch
Elizabeth Adams Wilson
anonymous
anonymous

CONTENTS

THE BASILICA NEIGHBORHOOD

Clockwise from top left:
Streetcars on Hennepin Avenue,
1946.
From the Parade Grounds, 1911.
Labor protest march, 1930s.
Christmas tree being set up,
1938.

This is a book of stories and voices that rise from one hundred years of the Basilica of Saint Mary of Minneapolis. In the fall of 1999, I took delivery of the first fat binder bulging with photographs and photocopies gathered by volunteer researchers at the Basilica and quickly submerged myself in the past of a small city block dominated by an enormous parish church. I have found myself, happily, in a sea of wonderful stories and details.

In the world rushing by on Hennepin Avenue, close regard is a rare commodity. Even if they have the inclination, even among the parishioners, few people have the time to really look. The Basilica of Saint Mary rewards the attentive with a wealth of detail that is at the same time beautiful and full of depth. The pleasure of this project has been to look carefully, and to retell the stories that have been told to me.

Imagine how the Basilica of Saint Mary must have towered over the younger, smaller city in 1914—commanding, graceful, adorned at the pediment with imagery of the Assumption of the Blessed Virgin into heaven, flanked by massive stone angels. One angel looks down toward the street, the other toward the sky, much like the parish itself.

On the west, the imposing rectory, once both home and workplace to the parish priests, still features back stairways to the dining room, and a front door where a person in need can knock and receive help. On the east side, the former convent, strictly sixties in architecture, is now a parish office building. Behind and a bit north, the school is still a school, although no longer filled with obedient Catholic children who walk in from the neighborhood. The Basilica block is urban and busy, filled with industry and purpose, populated day and night by people intending good in the world, and accomplishing it.

In the west tower hang six tremendous bells, representing voices of the saints of the Americas; Saint Elizabeth Ann Seton's voice rings out the hours each day. In the east tower, one can glimpse the now-silent, cracked bell that first hung in 1877 at the Basilica's predecessor parish, Immaculate Conception. Donated by the Total Abstinence societies of Minneapolis, it weighs three thousand pounds, and on its exterior is inscribed, in Latin, "May thy people called by me to this house of prayer be strengthened in the Lord." The rose window facing Hennepin Avenue pictures the patroness of the Basilica, the Enthroned Madonna and Child, in her distinctive blue, surrounded by three complete rows of angel faces—ranks of Seraphim, Cherubim, and Thrones. As the sun moves across the sky, the colors of the rose window travel through the sanctuary in the afternoon, illuminating pews and floors and worshipers.

In front of the Basilica stands the statue of Father Louis Hennepin, the Belgian missionary and explorer. Thousands of people attended its dedication on a windy Columbus Day in 1930, listening to Mass and sermon over loudspeakers outside a packed church. On the other side of the front steps stands the only fir tree on the Basilica grounds. It comes from the St. John's University woods, planted as part of a joint Christmas program in 1987. Even the iron handrails on the side entrances have a story—they were donated over sixty years ago by Miss Annie C. Quinlan, who thought it would be safer to have railings. Miss Quinlan and her sister Elizabeth were great friends, and frequent dinner partners, of pastor Monsignor James Michael Reardon. Members of that family have been in the parish from 1867 until the present day.

And, once you have opened the heavy bronze doors and

WEDDINGS AT THE BASILICA

Clockwise from top left:
Three sisters married in triple wedding, 1938.
Monsignor Reardon offers congratulations, 1956.
Note the statue from the Immaculate Conception parish, still at the Basilica, 1958.
On the steps, 1925.

passed through the narthex, with its curving ceiling and air of hushed transition, there is the vast interior. Most visitors pause there, just inside the door, gazing up, gazing ahead, tasting the air of peace, and community, and history. The street, suddenly, is far behind.

In the interior, the thematic continuity and depth of symbolism become more and more intricate. The baptismal font, decorated with the symbols of the four Evangelists, is located near the doors of the church to symbolize entry in the faith. Marian symbols—roses, lilies, intertwined letters A and M for Ave Maria—are in the windows, the walls, and in the ornate plaster ceiling. The crucifixion scene near the altar was modeled after a miraculous crucifix in Spain. It is missing the customary weeping Mary Magdalene figure. We, the onlookers, are meant to take her place. The upper rows of glorious windows tell the story of the life of the Blessed Virgin, all overseen by angels above.

Knowing and enjoying some of the stories that come from the Basilica's history can provide context and depth of appreciation for the casual observer of the building as well as for the parishioner. But what a visitor hears from a dark corner of the church when it is quiet is not the murmur of architecture. The echo you hear when the church is quiet is the sound of people.

The life of the community, in days and years, is made up of a long string of small events. Individual prayers, daily masses, the communion of children, drop-in visitors who sit quietly for a moment, a helping hand to someone in need: these are the small events that, over time, make up the strong web of faith and history that form the actual Basilica, as opposed to the physical one.

Individual actions, punctuated by occasional ceremony and shaped by faith, are the way in which an individual experiences the church, and looking back at what people have done in the parish over the years is one clear way of looking at its past. There are striking similarities between the earlier history of the parish and aspects of the Basilica today. In the same way that a closer

look at the Basilica's architectural detail yields a richer appreciation, a look at its history also reveals thematic continuity that seems both surprising and encouraging.

In his history *The Basilica of Saint Mary of Minneapolis: Historical and Descriptive Sketch*, Monsignor Reardon writes that early activities of the Immaculate Conception church included programs to help the needy, a parish library, public processions on St. Patrick's Day, and a leader, Father McGolrick, who became "one of the most prominent men of the town." McGolrick "joined many civic organizations," and "made his own the interests of the citizens." The Basilica of Saint Mary in the year 2000 is a church with tremendous social outreach programs; it has taken an active place in the public life of Minneapolis and made itself a stakeholder in its future. Rector Father Michael O'Connell and the parishioners have named a vision: "Seek the well-being of the city to which I have sent you. Pray for it to the Lord. For in seeking its well-being you shall find your own" (Jeremiah 29:7). This vision, and the programs that spring from it, are a natural evolution of the parish's longtime place in the city's affairs, and a response to the diverse character of its people.

In a 1966 church bulletin, one parishioner described the Basilica parish in terms that might be equally applicable today. "The Basilica is an intriguing conglomeration of the past and the future, beauty and ugliness, pathos and promise, young and old, wealth and poverty, decay and rejuvenation. To tackle the problems of the Basilica is to sample the problems facing modern America—education, poverty, racial integration, core city decay and renovation and a faceless, ever-changing population. But more importantly, it is to attempt a synthesis of the Church's role in these areas and to establish, by trial and error, pertinent and viable programs."

Because of the Basilica's location, its broad front steps have always been a good place to watch the civic life of Minneapolis.

FIRST COMMUNION

Clockwise from top left, photos date from 1951, 1955, 1995, undated, and 1911.

The archives hold a series of sketches and photographs in which the towering building remains the same while all the accoutrements change, from a horse and buggy to overhead streetcar lines to gleaming big-finned mid-century autos. From those steps, parishioners have watched modes of transportation change, labor unrest in the thirties, political parades, and celebrations for winning baseball teams.

The pastors, and later rectors, of the Basilica present another unbroken line of descent over the last hundred years. Particular periods of time are marked by the characteristics of the leadership, but one thing always remains the same. The number and variety of demands placed on the pastor are a matter for gape-mouthed awe. Pastors are in turn, or even simultaneously, called upon to be spiritual leaders, liturgists, administrators, professional men, representatives of the church in public life, fundraisers, planners, diplomats, confessors. They must also, by the way, write and deliver inspiring sermons, sometimes every week. In the late twentieth century, this was called multi-tasking. It is also called pastoral care.

It was never done alone, of course; there have been many assistant priests at the Basilica. Names through 1955 are included in Monsignor Reardon's book, but the archives today hold no complete list. Names occur in bulletins and parish records, signing off on weddings or baptisms. Parishioner scrapbooks contain fading snapshots of Father Doran or Monsignor Cullinan or Father Skrypek at picnics or farewell gatherings. Someone recalls a priest who used to play the guitar at the school, or someone who was especially kind. School children now grown remember their teachers better, providing glimpses of the Sisters of St. Joseph and later, the lay teachers at the Basilica School. In recent years, of course, lay ministers have been an important part of the Basilica's work.

Looking at its history makes it clear that the Basilica has always been an important church. Its leaders have come and gone from other key positions in the church hierarchy: important pastorships, diocesan offices, bishoprics, leadership posts in Catholic education. As one indication, the Basilica has continued to be a place where financial resources have been found, and spent. The old Church of the Immaculate Conception cost forty thousand dollars to build in 1872. The cost of the Basilica's exterior, with ground breaking in 1907, was close to one million dollars. In the 1990s, structural restoration and financing costs neared nine and a half million dollars.

From the very first, the church was the home for large and elaborate celebrations. Again and again in his book, Monsignor Reardon reports "thousands attending," a "packed church," for everything from formal ceremonies to May Day processions. The archives contain many photographs, some unmarked, of the grounds and the steps crowded with people, unidentified clergymen processing here and there, and the familiar view-from-the-gallery, featuring the tops of heads and the altar elaborately decorated. The scale of the building and its grounds, which can be surprisingly intimate in the sacristy or the apse, welcomes the masses; today's secular Block Parties, which can attract twenty thousand people, are the descendants of these earlier events.

The real story of continuity, however, is always with the families who have been involved with the parish over time, and over generations. For those, the Basilica is not only a civic monument, to be filled periodically with crowds and decorations and celebrations. For many families, it is their parish church, with all the intimacy and ownership and responsibility that that implies. Milestone events take place here—baptisms and first communions, confirmations and weddings and funerals—and these are sometimes recorded on film or by mementos like missals and scapulars and prayer cards. But the parish church is also the location of everyday worship. Sunday Masses, holy days, choir practices and church suppers and the recognition and celebration of the liturgical year. Advent and Christmas, Lent, Holy Week, Easter. These

AT THE BASILICA SCHOOL

Clockwise from top left:
Classroom at 11:00 A.M.,
about 1924.
Girls on the playground,
undated.
Class of 1957 in the school
gym.
The last eighth grade
graduating class, 1970.

make up the regular, and well-loved, rhythm of church life.

One aspect of the Basilica's past is by its very nature not well represented by archival materials. From the very beginning of the parish, through all the pastors and the building projects and the passage of decades, music has been an important part of life at the Basilica. At the very first Mass in the new building, on May 31, 1914, "the responses of the Mass were sung by an augmented choir with organ and orchestral accompaniment." By 1922, the church had hired a professional musician, John Jacob Beck, to lead its music program. A fine organist and musician, Beck formed the first vested boy's choir in the diocese. Again in the sixties, the Basilica's music program flourished, with three choirs and no less than three organs in the building. And for the last twenty years of the century, music and performance programs have been an integral part of liturgy and celebration at the Basilica. When looking at photos of the past, largely posed choirs and sternly-robed choirmasters, it is necessary to listen hard, to imagine a faint but ongoing thread of sacred music underlying it all.

The turn of the twenty-first century is a golden age for the Basilica of Saint Mary. Growth, activity and engagement characterize its last ten years. Purpose and commitment define its future. A long range planning committee, commissioned by the Parish Council, identified six core values to serve as a guide for daily parish activity, and to describe the character and culture of the parish. Those values are: Spirituality, Hospitality, Diversity, Respect, Stewardship, and Community. The Basilica calls itself, and properly so, a traditional church with a modern message.

Long time parishioners have told me that they see something new every time they come into the church, and there is certainly much to see. A historically-minded visitor, by squinting slightly, can blur the edges of the contemporary crowd and glimpse earlier Sunday mornings, bathed in light from the windows and filled with the sound of music. Clothing changes, manners change, rules and habits change, but people still come up the steps from the street and enter the church seeking and finding a living community of faith.

To some extent, exploring the Basilica's history is a process of examining traces of the past that happen to rise to the surface of the present. It is an imperfect and ongoing endeavor. Dipping in and looking hard, however, is a rich business. It reminds us that we are only part of a long line of people whose attention has been drawn and held by this magnificent place—a line that stretches from the past, through our time, and into the undetermined future.

—*Peg Guilfoyle*

"As a writing man, or secretary, I have always felt charged with the safekeeping of all unexpected items of worldly or unworldly enchantment. as though I might be held personally responsible if even a small one were to be lost."

—*E.B. White*

Monsignor Reardon writes in his history of the Basilica that the shed church, right, was "provided with altar, benches, and furnishings of the most primitive kind." An anonymous writer for the Catholic Bulletin wrote years later that "it was a humble beginning—so rude and humble that the new church was called 'the shed.' But to the pioneers it meant much. They had their own priest to provide for their spiritual wants; they had their own little school where their children could go to receive instruction in the three R's and in their faith."

The photograph below, printed in the Catholic Bulletin *on the occasion of the Basilica's opening in 1914, shows the first band organized by the choir of the Immaculate Conception church, circa 1870. The photo was taken "at the first picnic held by the parish." Note Father McGolrick seated at far right. The large upright horns are instruments from Civil War era bands.*

*C*atholics arrived in Minnesota and, like other pioneers, brought their faith practices with them. Creating lives in a new land—shelter, food, community, commerce— they also had to build the infrastructure of their religion.

Starting small, with pioneer priests and home observances, the religious infrastructure grew with the Minnesota Territory, not of its own volition, but as a result of the small choices and actions that many Catholics, clergy, laity and leaders, made over many years. At the time, laying down the roots of faith in a new land surely must have seemed slow and perhaps difficult to discern. But looking back now, we are able to see that each small individual action, each act of faith and building, led to the next, in the same way that a stonemason lays the first course of a wall.

Although the Reverend James Michael Reardon would not become the pastor of the Basilica until 1921, he appears in its story much earlier, as its student and historian. Monsignor Reardon's writings provide much of what we know about the Basilica's beginnings.

*The Immaculate Conception
School in 1912.*

AT THE BASILICA	LIFE OF THE CHURCH	CIVIC LIFE
		1848 First settlers arrive at St. Anthony.
1850		1849 Minnesota becomes a territory.
1860		1858 Minnesota becomes the 32nd state.
1868 October, Immaculate Conception parish founded with Father James McGolrick as pastor; construction of "shed" church begins.		1865 End of American Civil War.
1870		1867 City of Minneapolis incorporated.
1873 January 1, Dedication of the second Immaculate Conception church.	1884 Bishop Thomas Langdon Grace dies; succeeded by Archbishop John Ireland. Diocese of St. Paul becomes Archdiocese of St. Paul.	1870 First gas lights in Minneapolis. Population of Minneapolis is 13,066.
1889 Father James C. Byrne becomes pastor.		
1890 1892 Father James J. Keane becomes pastor.		
1900		
1902 Father Thomas E. Cullen becomes pastor.	1903 Pope Leo XIII dies; succeeded by Pope Pius X.	1900 Population of Minneapolis is 202,718. Average U.S. income is $438 per year. Loaf of bread costs 5¢.
		1904 New state Capitol completed in St. Paul.

Father McGolrick rented lodgings or lived with other priests and parishioners until the purchase and refitting of the first rectory, shown below, in 1874.

Monsignor Reardon gives this brief account of the founding of Immaculate Conception parish, the predecessor to the Basilica of Saint Mary, in his book The Catholic Church in the Diocese of St. Paul, *enlivening the recital of facts with a story that reminds us that our historic leaders had their human sides as well.*

"Owing to the rapid growth in the population of Minneapolis, as the nascent town was named in 1855, a new parish became a necessity and, in October, 1868, the Bishop [Bishop Thomas Grace] authorized the Reverend James McGolrick, recently ordained in Ireland and stationed at the Cathedral, [the predecessor to the present-day Cathedral of Saint Paul], to found a parish under the aegis of the Immaculate Conception of the Blessed Virgin Mary. In the rear of the school, but opening into it by folding doors, Father McGolrick erected a frame building, known as the 'shed church,' which served the congregation as a house of worship until replaced by a stone edifice on Third Street at Third Avenue North, the cornerstone of which was blessed and placed in position by Bishop Grace on July 9, 1871, and which was dedicated on New Year's Day of 1873.

"The Bishop had promised to officiate on that occasion but when the time came he refused to attend the ceremony because of the manner in which the town had been placarded with posters announcing the event—a form of publicity to which he strenuously objected. In his absence, Father Tissot of St. Anthony blessed the church and Father Ireland [later Archbishop Ireland] preached the sermon."

Monsignor Reardon describes McGolrick as "youthful, energetic, learned and devoted"; the accomplishments listed certainly bear that description out. Father McGolrick is reported to have organized a Saint Vincent de Paul conference "to care for the needy members of the flock," the Father Mathew Total Abstinence Society, a parish circulating library of five hundred volumes, bazaars, and a Saint Patrick's Day celebration that included processions and plays. He also gave public lectures on historical and scientific topics "which were listened to by huge and appreciative audiences." These are the distant forerunners of today's outreach programs at the Basilica of Saint Mary.

All this activity was centered in the old church, the "shed church," which must have been a burgeoning community institution. When the cornerstone was laid for the new Immaculate Conception in 1871, Monsignor Reardon reports that the bishop preached a sermon to a congregation of nearly three thousand persons, from a temporary pulpit on the foundation of the new church "which had been floored and decorated for the occasion."

No doubt some of those three thousand had been attracted by the procession that preceded the event. The bishop's carriage from Saint Paul was met "at the suspension bridge" and escorted to the church by several chapters of parish organizations, along with the Emerald Band.

With his unfailing interest in history and continuity, Monsignor Reardon reports that two acolytes in that ceremony, James C.

According to Monsignor Reardon's history of the Basilica, the second church of the Immaculate Conception, with its cornerstone laid in 1871, was planned to be "not only the handsomest but the largest church in Minneapolis." The church stood at Third Street and Third Avenue North, until it was razed in 1922.

Church of Immaculate Conception, Minneapolis.

The Basilica site's most colorful use was under the ownership of one "Fish" Jones, described as a "zoo entrepreneur," who had "a large tract" of property that included Sixteenth and Hennepin. "He moved his menagerie there, and continued to add to it until, to accommodate all his birds and beasts, he fenced in his whole yard right down to Hennepin Avenue." A

contemporary publication says twenty varieties of pigeons and seven varieties of pheasants were available for sale there. It was reported years later that "nearby property owners registered strong complaints pertaining to noise and objectionable odors." Perhaps Mr. Jones decided to sell. Or perhaps, as Monsignor Reardon prefers, Jones never owned, but only rented the property. There is a parish story, perhaps apocryphal, about Mr. Jones parading his animals off the property to make way for the new occupants. All accounts agree, however, on this point: Fish Jones, "as an advertisement," always dressed in a top hat and Prince Albert coat.

Byrne and Patrick J. Danehy, would be the first parish boys to enter the priesthood. And with his keen reportorial eye, he tells a small tale about the dedication two years later. Bishop Grace, as we know, was not there, and Father Ireland was preaching.

"In the excitement of the moment, he forgot to announce the collection—a serious oversight! When he stepped from the pulpit Father McGolrick rushed to him and called his attention to the fact, and Father Ireland returned to the pulpit and made adequate amends for the omission."

Father McGolrick was succeeded as pastor by the Reverend

James C. Byrne who "accomplished a great deal" for the parish's "temporal and spiritual well-being." When Father Byrne assumed the presidency of the Seminary of St. Thomas Aquinas in September 1892, the Immaculate Conception parish was led by Father James J. Keane. Monsignor Reardon reports that the church facilities were improved during Father Keane's day, and he must have been a forward thinker.

"During the latter years of his residence in the parish he became convinced of the need of a new and more modern church in another locality. The growth of the city and the changes necessitated by commercial expansion made it evident that the new edifice would have to be built at some distance from the old site. The locality about the church was more and

L.S. DONALDSON COMPANY
MINNEAPOLIS, MINN.

L.S. DONALDSON
PRESIDENT.

May 9th, 1911.

Most Reverend John Ireland,
    Archbishop of the Diocese of St. Paul,
        St. Paul, Minnesota.

My dear Archbishop:

        In reference to our conversation of
the other day in regard to the lots that you
have purchased, and will require for Pro-
Cathedral purposes.

        I have talked the matter over with
my wife, who understands everything clearly,
and I desire and hope to be able to take care
of this property after two years.   It is my
wish to donate to the church any land in that
block needed for Pro-Cathedral purposes.

        Very Respectfully,

        Lawrence S. Donaldson

Reverend Thomas E. Cullen, pastor of Immaculate Conception during the planning and building of the Basilica of Saint Mary.

more given over to wholesale houses and manufacturing plants; and the people who resided therein were forced to move to outlying districts and, perforce, the church must follow them."

Elsewhere, Reardon said even more bluntly "that the Immaculate Conception Church became an oasis in a Sahara of warehouses."

Several sites were considered for the new church. Father Keane bought the first at Ninth Street and present-day LaSalle Avenue. It was too small and was later sold.

The second prospect was acquired during the pastorship of Father Thomas E. Cullen, who had been ordained less than one

year when he began to lead Immaculate Conception in 1902. Ordained by former pastor and then Bishop of Duluth James McGolrick, Father Cullen was a man who "spent himself for the young people of the city. He popularized early Communion for children. His beautiful sermons were adapted to the minds of little ones. His children's Masses became so popular that adults overcrowded the several churches he served and special arrangements had to be made for the accommodation of the young."

In 1904, six lots at the corner of Hawthorn Avenue and Thirteenth Street were purchased as a site for a new church. Later on, they were "deemed unsuitable." Lawrence S. Donaldson, a "prominent merchant and a member of the parish," purchased and then donated seven lots at Sixteenth Street and Hennepin Avenue. The site had been found.

"Rise then, Pro-Cathedral, rise quickly
above the foundations, and be to us,
more by far than a noble monument of granite
and marble; be to us the house of God,
the vestibule of Heaven."

—*Archbishop John Ireland at the laying
of the cornerstone*

Far left: Architect Emmanuel Masqueray.

Left: Archbishop John Ireland, the first Archbishop of Saint Paul, commissioned both the Basilica of Saint Mary and the Cathedral of Saint Paul at nearly the same time. Born in Ireland in 1838, he was ordained to the priesthood in St. Paul in 1861. One of his early assistants in Minnesota was a young Father James Michael Reardon, who remained a lifelong admirer. On the Ireland memorial in the back of the Basilica are words that Monsignor Reardon might have written: "A great prelate who in his days pleased God and wrought wonderful things for the church."

Below: Archbishop Ireland speaks to crowds at the ground-breaking ceremony in 1907.

BUILDING THE BASILICA
1907–1913

*I*t is a tremendous act of faith to build something like the Basilica—faith and grand vision, a large measure of hard-nosed practicality, and a certain willful blindness to obstacles and hardships.

In the early part of the century, under the vigorous leadership of Archbishop John Ireland, the small Catholic community of Minneapolis undertook the erection of an enormous church that would be a landmark to the faithful and a statement to the rest. We are here, the building would say.

Looking back at formally-posed black and white photographs of the founders, the builders, and the architects, we tend to view the process as the final sum of its efforts. They were giants, we say. They built it, we say, and it opened in such and such a year. But it is worth remembering that the raising of the Basilica was as laborious and complex an effort as any contemporary civic effort is today. It required leadership and included grand events like the laying of cornerstones. But it also surely required the small events that history forgets: subscription lists, sermons urging donations, and committee meetings that lasted long into the night. It included people who got their way and those who, disgruntled, did not. People dug deep into their personal pockets and watched with pride, as the mighty building rose up. Children played on the construction site and the whole city watched.

"It was a remarkable thing. I don't know whether any archbishop in the history of the United States, or in fact the world, ever built two cathedrals at the same time, as Ireland did. And he was an old man then!"
—Historian Joseph B. Connors, a member of the Basilica parish from 1923 "until the war years."

"On Sunday, May 31, 1908, the whole population of Minneapolis awoke with one thought—the cornerstone of the new Pro-Cathedral of Saint Mary was that day to be laid. Thousands of visitors had come to the city. Parishes in all parts of the diocese had sent delegations to take part in the parade. Thousands of others were attracted by curiosity to be eyewitnesses of the great event where so many distinguished clergymen and statesmen were to be seen and heard. The churches were crowded to the doors at the early Masses, everyone planning to be downtown in time to see the parade form for the march to the Pro-Cathedral grounds." Thirty thousand Catholics marched that day, according to the Catholic Bulletin's memorial edition, edited by Father James Michael Reardon.

AT THE BASILICA	LIFE OF THE CHURCH	CIVIC LIFE

1900

1908 May 31, Cornerstone laid,
      Pro-Cathedral of Saint Mary.

1910

| | | 1910 Population of Minneapolis is 301,408. Average U.S. income is $574 per year. Quart of milk costs 8.5 ¢. |

1913 August, Pro-Cathedral School opens.   1914 Pope Pius X dies; succeeded by Pope Benedict XV.   1914 World War I breaks out in Europe.

1915

Architectural historian Carol Frenning joined the Basilica of Saint Mary in 1975 and "has been a person in the pew there ever since." She is particularly interested in Emmanuel Masqueray and his work.

"I really think the Basilica is one of his finer examples. He was an important architect, and this is one of the finest examples of Beaux Arts architecture in this area.

"It's a very refined design, an interesting use of classical detailing in a creative kind of way. And it's a building that was meant to be as up to date as possible. Minnesota was only fifty years from statehood when they started, so I've heard tales of people sitting on the steps of the Basilica as it was being constructed, and watching prairie schooners over near Loring Pond. They were still homesteading in the Dakotas, so there's a real dichotomy between the kind of vision and foresight that was behind creating this huge building, and the newness of the whole territory. Here in the middle of nowhere.

"One of the things that always surprises people is that it looks like it's a masonry-constructed building, but in fact it was very advanced technologically; it's a steel and concrete interior construction. It was a building that used the latest technology but tried to capture the older look. It was said to have the widest nave of any church in the world when it was built. It is eighty-two feet from pillar to pillar and 140 feet long. The ceiling height of the nave is seventy-five feet, and it is supported by five

Commemorative medal from the laying of the cornerstone.

NEW CATHEDRAL, MINNEAPOLIS, MINN.

This postcard, marked "New
Cathedral, Minneapolis, Minn."
pre-dates construction, and demonstrates how some of the design
changed during the process. It shows
a round dome with four columns surrounding it. The finished building
does not have those columns, and the
dome is square, or lantern-shaped.

main pillars, marking off each bay. The pillars support five major
steel girders that go across the top, and that was the way in
which they were able to construct this large volume of space.

"Now the choice of that kind of style was not only because
of the French architect. There's history there. Catholics weren't
allowed to build cathedrals until late, after the American
Revolution. And there was a very conscious decision made at
that time to choose a classical style for the Church of Rome, in
order to distinguish it from the Protestant churches. So the
Basilica certainly fits in with that American tradition, choosing
that kind of architect and architecture.

"But Masqueray was a French architect, and he never lived
in Minnesota. He came from a much milder climate and we
have these tremendous temperature shifts in our climate. The

Basilica dome leaked, but all of Masqueray's domes leak. I've had
architects from all over calling me about that, and the first thing
they say is 'Does your dome leak?'

"One of the main tenets of Beaux Arts architecture is that a
building should follow its program; it should look like what it is.
That's certainly a response you frequently get from people who
come to tour the building: it really looks like the way a church
should look. That was certainly a conscious intention by the
architect.

"The ceiling which covers the main nave area is made out of
carved and molded plaster. Some of it is up to twelve inches
deep. It's a very specialized technique for making a plaster ceiling. Imbedded in it, you'll see designs that refer to Mary, particularly Ave Maria, the AM, and the shell and floral motifs."

Symbols of the Blessed Virgin, known as Marian designs, abound throughout the church. Reardon lists those in friezes beneath the windowsills: Dove, Tower of David, Pomegranate, Sun, Lily, Fleur-de-lis, Rose, Star, Three Lilies, Pierced Heart.

One of Frenning's favorite stories, often repeated by Sunday morning tour guides, is that Archbishop Ireland directed his architect to make the domes of both the Basilica and the Cathedral of Saint Paul stand just a bit higher than the dome of the Minnesota State Capitol, then under construction.

"Well, it's even more pronounced in St. Paul because, for years, you would drive into town and the three highest towers would be the Cathedral, the State Capitol, and the First National Bank. So you had God, man, and money laid out right there.

"It was very apparent to me that in the beginning this was a very fashionably important place in which to worship. It was one of the premiere churches along Hennepin Avenue, which really held the churches that everybody wanted to belong to."

Above: Architect's rendering of the Basilica's intended interior.

Above left: This photo is marked "Cathedral of Saint Mary being built. Boys from De LaSalle."

Above: Plaster sculptor Adolfo Minuti.

Right: The Minuti Studio on University Avenue. Adolfo Minuti at far left.

Victoria Barlow Keith's family was heavily involved in the creation of the Basilica.

"My great grandfather Adolfo Minuti and grandfather Augusto, great uncle Torello and other great uncle Lorenzo were Italian plaster sculptors who practiced their craft first in Italy and then in Minneapolis and St. Paul in the early 1900s. The Minuti family and the Brioschi-Minuti Company created the spectacular ornate Italianate decorative plaster ceilings and interiors of most of the area's significant structures created during that time, including the Basilica of Saint Mary."

Sometimes the community leaders of the past are only names in dusty paperwork. Kathleen McCarthy Jewett remembers a little more, as a part of her own family history. As a small child, she was told her grandfather W. P. Devereux, who chaired the building committee, had built the Basilica. She laughs now, remembering her impression that, in addition to running his own grain company, he was also a stonemason on the side. It was a long time before she thought to ask if he hadn't had any help building the big church.

The Pro-Cathedral School was built immediately adjacent to the Basilica as the church neared completion. Monsignor Reardon says only that "it became evident that a new parochial school in the vicinity was necessary," and gives the school only passing attention in his history of the Basilica, although in community life, a school building houses as much human activity as a church, and sometimes more. The school was completed in only one year—open for occupancy in August 1913—and was paid off in 1914, the same year of the "informal opening" of the new church.

The building was thoroughly modern and, importantly, housed the underground boiler room that supplied heat for all the parish buildings. The pupils, Monsignor Reardon writes, assisted at Mass in the third floor auditorium until the Pro-Cathedral was finished. They heard the very first (as opposed to the official first) Mass in the church at 9 A.M. on May 31, 1914.

Left: Two columns in the Catholic Bulletin list contributors—and their donation amounts down to one dollar—to the fund for the beautification of the grounds.

The choir of the Pro-Cathedral of Saint Mary on Easter Sunday 1917, with Father Cullen seated at center. Easter finery and bonnets abound. This large group may be the "augmented" choir which had been referred to in earlier accounts, perhaps drawing members from other parishes.

- Choir -
- Pro Cathedral of
Easter Sunday - 1917

*A*fter a house is built, you move into it. A long series of occasions attended the rising of the Basilica—the ground-breaking, the cornerstone, the long building process, civic dedication, first Mass, solemn dedication—and each marked a phase toward the completion of the structure. After the ceremonies and the processions are over, and after the bishop goes home, it's a parish with a mighty big church.

With its unfinished interior, cement walls, and plain glass windows, the brand-new Basilica must have been cavernous and, in the winter, cold. With the new school and the new rectory on Laurel Avenue, the parish had several buildings to support. Still, it was a big parish, including both the prosperous residential areas of Kenwood and Lake of the Isles and working class families from just north and west. There was a choir and, during World War I, the parish ladies gathered for Red Cross work. Even though the war interrupted plans to finish the interior, community life went on.

In 1919, Father Cullen described the parish boundaries: "On the north, the Mississippi River. On the south, Lake Street. On the east, Seventh Avenue South to Grant Street to Vine Place to Franklin Avenue to Harriet Avenue to Lake Street. On the west, Twelfth Avenue North."

AT THE BASILICA	LIFE OF THE CHURCH	CIVIC LIFE
1910		
1914 May 31, First Mass celebrated at Pro-Cathedral.		
1915		
1915 August 15, Dedication of Pro-Cathedral.		1915 Average U.S. income is $633 per year. Loaf of bread costs 6.1¢.
	1918 Archbishop Ireland dies; succeeded by Archbishop Austin Dowling.	1917 U.S. declares war on Germany, joins World War I.
1920		1918 End of World War I.

Monsignor Reardon describes parish work during World War I.

with the stamp of death on the fields of France and elsewhere, while others came through the fiery ordeal with maimed bodies and shell-shocked minds—mere wrecks of the vigorous manhood and buoyant strength with which they marched away so proudly at their country's call.

"A center for organized war work, under the direction of the Red Cross, was established in the parish school and there the women met to do their bit. They prepared surgical dressings, hospital garments, comfort kits, knitted articles—sweaters, socks, caps, etc.—and sent packages to the boys in service at home and 'over there.' They furnished garments for refugees, adopted French war orphans and participated in the food conservation campaign.

"The parishioners, both men and women, bought Liberty Bonds, Thrift and War Savings Stamps, contributed to the War Chest and Knights of Columbus fund, and actively participated in 'drives' for these and other purposes. Not a few took part in the program for Americanization in the schools and elsewhere and helped to educate foreign groups in the principles of American citizenship. Thus, by manpower, money, supplies and personal service did the people of the parish help the United States to 'make the world safe for democracy.'"

Left: Basilica interior during Advent 1914. Note the original altar, the raw, unfinished walls, wooden communion railing, temporary light fixture, and the absence of stained glass windows. The only interior furnishings that remain today are the pews.

"When, on April 6, 1917, Congress declared that a state of war existed between the United States and the Imperial German government, the Pro-Cathedral parish entered seriously and whole-heartedly into the task of aiding Uncle Sam in his efforts to further the cause of the Allies. Father Cullen exhorted the people from pulpit and platform to do all they could to sustain the morale of the boys who joined the colors.

"The available records for the first World War show a roster of 490 men in the different branches of the service and four nurses. Many of the former sealed their patriotism

A corner in nearby downtown Minneapolis, 1913. Note early public transportation at the extreme left, automobiles, and horse-drawn carriage on the right.

Below: The second parish rectory built the next year.

In June 1914, the clergy moved to a new house on Laurel Avenue, one of two on a site in the rear of the Pro-Cathedral. After the houses were demolished in 1928, the lots were merged into the schoolyard. The priests of the Pro-Cathedral also "attended" other churches and chapels, such as the chapels of Saint Margaret's Academy, a day school for girls, Holy Angels Academy, and the City of Minneapolis workhouse. Mass was also celebrated at the old Immaculate Conception church for a few years.

The solemn dedication of the Pro-Cathedral of Saint Mary was held on August 15, 1915, the feast of the Assumption of the Blessed Virgin Mary.

Left: The War Memorial Chalice.

"At the end of the first World War, the people of the parish gave of their gold ornaments and precious stones to be incorporated into the 'Liberty Chalice' as a thanksgiving offering. On December 21, 1932, it was enriched by the addition of two diamonds from earrings donated by Mrs. Mary McLaughlin, matron of the cafeteria for many years." After Monsignor Reardon's report in 1955, the chalice was renamed the War Memorial Chalice. Today, it is commonly used at Sunday Eucharist.

Monsignor Reardon, in his history of the Basilica, relates that "the altar is the gift, not of any society or group, but of about fifteen hundred parishioners whose names are sealed in a glass tube enclosed in a bronze reliquary embedded beneath the sepulchre of the mensa, or altar table, containing the relics of Saints Aurelia and Victoria, martyrs." The Basilica's patroness stands atop the baldachino above a plaque that reads "Mater Divinae Gratiae" (Mother of Divine Grace).

F ather James Michael Reardon's arrival in 1921 began a pastorship of four decades. Many stories about Father Reardon survive him; it is clear that he was a strong leader, and he began to demonstrate this immediately, moving to have the Pro-Cathedral declared a Basilica, hiring a professional musician to lead the music program, and undertaking to finish the interior of his vast and no doubt drafty church. Committees met, lists were drawn up. Coffers were filled and emptied.

This time, though, the original architect was gone. Emmanuel Masqueray had died in 1917. The overall plan for finishing the interior was surely guided by the pastor, with whomever he chose to consult. In a story about the stained glass windows, the Minneapolis Times *called them "the results of a carefully thought out Christian scheme by Father James Reardon." The same might be said of the entire beautiful interior. In detail, in symbolism, in rich materials, in thematic continuity, close examination of the Basilica's interior yields rich results.

During the same time, a fine school and a grand new rectory were completed. By the end of the Roaring Twenties, the Basilica must have fully looked its part as the leading place of Catholic worship on the west side of the Mississippi.

Still, parish life went on. Small children, dressed in their best, entered the school and received good education from the nuns and their report cards by hand from Father Reardon. They walked in from the neighborhood, learned to be altar boys, competed in essay contests, and watched Minneapolis civic life from the front steps of the Basilica.

Above: A 1923 photo shows the Benziger Brothers Studio in Italy. On November 3, the company wrote Father Reardon: "The first shipment of marble for your altar is being loaded on the steamer that will leave Leghorn, Italy, within the next few days. It is, of course, a slow steamer, and is due in New York about December 5."

"So much of the Basilica is shaped by Monsignor Reardon. In a way, all of us live in his shadow. From 1921 to 1963, he almost singularly defined the nature of this church."
—Father Michael O'Connell

View from Kenwood Water Tower, 1927.

AT THE BASILICA	LIFE OF THE CHURCH	CIVIC LIFE

1920

1921   August, Father James Michael Reardon
        becomes pastor.

1923–1926 *Pro-Cathedral interior finished.*
1927–1926 *Construction of sacristy and rectory.*

1922   *Pope Benedict XV dies; succeeded by
        Pope Pius XI.*

1920   *Population of Minneapolis is 380,582.
        Average U.S. income is $1,407 per year.
        Loaf of bread costs 11.7¢.*
1922   *First radio station in Minneapolis begins
        broadcasting.*

1925

1926   *February 1, Pro-Cathedral name changed to
        Basilica of Saint Mary.*

1929   *March 26, Requiem Mass for Marshall Foch.*

1926   *First commercial air flight from Minneapolis
        to Chicago.*
1929   *Foshay Tower completed.*
1929   *Stock market crashes; Great Depression begins.*

1930

Father James Michael Reardon.

ather James M. Reardon was the pastor of the Church of Saint Mary in St. Paul, and the Editor-in-Chief of the Catholic Bulletin when he was called to the Pro-Cathedral in 1921 by the Most Reverend Archbishop Dowling. Father Cullen went on to the presidency of the College of Saint Thomas. Looking back now, some themes seem to recur through the decades of his leadership. His writing skills and his interest in history combined in a detailed history of the Basilica and later, a history of the diocese. He was a note-taker. The archives possess book upon book of parish records in his careful hand, the handwriting devolving over time. Sister Genevieve Schillo, who taught in the Basilica School in the early sixties, remembers that he was a charter member of the Catholic Historical Society and a faithful member of the Priests Total Abstinence League. Among his many honors, she says, was this interesting one: "Upon finishing the interior of Basilica church and assuring that it was fully paid for, he was named Irremovable Rector, a title no longer in favor!"

He must have been interested in music. Only one year after his appointment, he hired John Jacob Beck, a very fine musician and organist, to direct the parish music programs.

Father Reardon was known as a stern and pious man, and a man concerned with frugality. In his history of the Basilica, not two pages after referring to the beginning of his pastorship, Father Reardon begins talking about his first great task, to finish the interior of the big church. First, he gives the financial report of what he found at the parish, and then goes on to record his first proposed solution. "Before actual finishing operations began the pastor announced that, if one-third of the parishioners would pledge a dollar a Sunday for four years, the total cost would be paid in full without recourse to assessments, special collections, bazaars, festivals, bingo or pink teas. The suggestion was not accepted and as a result the indebtedness was not paid for nearly twenty years."

But he did pay it. Father Reardon established a habit of frugality in the parish that would last for decades, but it was frugality in the midst of the creation of an architectural and artistic splendor. "Painting and sculpture," he said, "are twin handmaids of religion, and the Church employs them in her liturgy and in the decoration of her temples."

The ornamental grillwork surrounding the altar was made by Flour City Metal in Minneapolis. Note the Bishop's Throne at left, circa 1926.

Completion of the church's interior began in 1923, only two years after Father Reardon became the pastor. Architectural historian Carol Frenning tells the tale.

"The choice of subject matter, the sculptural programs and placements, were all very much up to date. They were sort of the hot Catholic topics and saints of the day. Saint Theresa and Saint John Vianney had just been canonized fairly recently; it was a way of saying we're modern and we have the latest saints!

"The work in the interior was overseen by the local architectural firm of Abrams and Slifer, who took over Masqueray's practice after he died in 1917. The high altar and baldachin, its permanent ornamental canopy, were designed by the firm of McGinnis and Walsh of Boston. The paintings on tapestry of the four evangelists in the sanctuary dome were completed by Libbey and Libbey of Minneapolis, under the supervision of Thomas Gaytee, who also designed and executed the stained glass windows."

Some of the artwork was created to be seen from below.

"That's a function of two things. One is the physicality of the building. Something is high up and you're looking up at it, so it has to be designed in a way that you'll perceive it as a whole. So it's often tipped if it's a sculpture or distorted if it's a painting or a window painting. Then there are specific layers that would be associated with earth and with heavenly paradise. In the Basilica windows, for example, the lowest level, in the ambulatory areas, are Old Testament figures whose story relates to the story that's up above, the New Testament. That's a very traditional way of showing the supplanting of the old, with the new on top of it. Then above those windows are angels in roundels with the litany of Loretto written on them—that was a popular devotional prayer at the time. Up there, that's the heavenly sphere.

"It's a fascinating thing that, with the windows, we have a complete program intact. There is a theme and a story that's told in the connections of all the windows as you go around. They're all interrelated; they were thought through as a program, and a way of teaching. There is a unity in them. It would have been Father Reardon's ideas.

The windows tell the story of the Blessed Mother. The western rose window begins the story, representing the Immaculate Conception of the Blessed Virgin. Her Glorious Coronation in Heaven finishes on the east, in a rose window commissioned and dedicated by the League of Catholic Women. Encircling these two groups of figures are the first three of the nine choirs of Angels, the ones nearest to the Throne of God, the Seraphim, Cherubim and Thrones. Starting on the Gospel side of the nave, near the pulpit, moments from Mary's life are represented in almost-chronological order. The windows place Mary's marriage to Joseph before the Annunciation of the Angel Gabriel, a reversal of the order of events as they appear in the Bible. It is said that the two events were reversed because the parish—or perhaps Father Reardon—thought it

improper to depict Mary as an unwed mother.

The upper windows, in order, were listed in the newspaper in 1926. On the ambulatory level below, the windows depict prophets and apostles whose stories relate to the window above. Below the Nativity of Our Lord is the prophet Micheas. "And thou Bethlehem, out of thee shall he come forth unto me that is to be ruler in Israel."

The Marriage of the Blessed Virgin—Prophet, Raguel
The Annunciation of the Blessed Virgin—Prophet, Isaias
The Visitation of the Blessed Virgin—Prophetess, Anna
The Nativity of our Lord—Prophet, Micheas
The Adoration of the Magi—Prophet, Balaam
The Presentation in the Temple—Prophet, Malachias
The Flight into Egypt—Prophet, Jacob
The Holy Family—Prophet, Moses
Our Lord in the Temple—Saint Luke, the Evangelist
The Death of Saint Joseph—Prophet, Solomon

Continuing on Epistle side, opposite to the pulpit
The Marriage at Cana—Saint John, the Evangelist
The Saviour meets His Mother—Prophetess, Rachel
The Crucifixion of our Lord—Prophet, Amos
The Descent from the Cross—Prophet, Zacharias
The Deposition—Prophet, Jeremias
The Entombment of our Lord—Prophet, Jonas
The Return from Calvary—Prophet, Joseph of Arimathea
The Apparition of our Lord to His Blessed Mother—
    Prophet, Abraham
The Pentecost—Prophetess, Judith
The Death of the Blessed Virgin—Prophet, Saint Peter

In all the windows, the Blessed Virgin is easily recognized by the distinctive shade of blue reserved for her.

"The windows on the west side of the Basilica are just marvelous. On sunset days, the windows turn deep and beautiful oranges and yellows and then, as the sunset draws to a close, it's like it soaks up a blue green liquid from the bottom. It fills up the entire window until they fade to black. It's the most fabulous thing."
—Jay Hunstiger

Sister-in-law Anne Neubauer loves to tell Florence's story.

"The way I remember the story is when she was six years old, around 1909, a neighbor had a very beautiful home with a stained glass window in it, and she fell in love with stained glass. But when she went to the Minneapolis College of Art and Design, there was no glass painting as such, so she took sculpture. After she left college, she started working at Gaytee Studios. And she was the only woman there for a long time."

There were other women at Gaytee by 1946, when Florence's co-workers created a little booklet as a gift for her. In it, they describe her bright blue smock and helpful air. There are sketches of Florence at her "big glass easel," and perched on a stepladder painting with a fistful of brushes. Florence Neubauer was a member of the parish and attended church with her family every Sunday and Holy Day, bathed in the light of the windows she'd helped to create.

"She was very analytical about the windows; where the average person wouldn't possibly notice something, she would see it. She put in a lot of her own time on the Basilica windows. And then she worked again on restoring the windows. There was some vandalism to the windows in the 1960s. Florence repainted some of the inscription plates during the repair. She became very ill with cancer, and then went into remission. You would never believe the dedication and the love she had for her work. She went to work when you would think the wind would blow her over, she was so frail. She never married; her work was everything, just everything for her.

"As time went on, she tried very hard to get students, to train them. And they'd get just so far and then they'd quit. It was just terrible because she would say, 'Who's going to do this when I'm not here?'"

Historian Joseph B. Connors was a schoolboy in the Basilica parish in the twenties.

"My own memories of the Basilica begin in the year 1923. My parents had been in the original old Immaculate Conception parish, and I recall my mother telling how she attended the laying of the cornerstone for the Basilica. She and my sister Alice remained members of the parish down into the 1960s, and I was a member until the war years when I went into the Army. It was a close relationship over a considerable period of time.

"We lived in the middle of a row of five large apartment buildings close by, so when I'd look out my front window as a little boy, I'd be looking right up at the huge cross of the church. I used to study it through my telescope. Later we moved to Bryn Mawr, near Laurel and Newton. I'd walk to school over the Bryn Mawr bridge.

"It was a very interesting setting for the church. It was sur-rounded, of course, by a neighborhood, by houses. Directly across from the corner of the Basilica, opposite the school, were two apartment buildings called the Cathedral Apartments. The girl I later married lived in there when she was a little girl. And then there were frame houses; it was a working class neighborhood, heavily populated, surrounding the church. It was an extraordinary parish, because it was so huge. You had kids that came, and I suppose they walked to school in all weathers, from as far up as Sixth Avenue North, a couple of miles away. On the other hand there were wealthy kids that came from the Lake of the Isles district. It made an interesting and highly democratic mixture for the school population because what happened in the classroom depended on talent, not whether they came from a poor family or a rich family.

Above: The combined fifth and sixth grade class at Basilica School, 1925. Joseph Connors is in the front row, second from right.

DIPLOMA

This Certifies

That _Rose Piazza_

has completed the Course of Study prescribed by

Pro-Cathedral School of Saint Mary

and having passed a satisfactory examination,
is entitled to this Diploma.

Given at Minneapolis, Minnesota, this _4th_ day of _June_ _1922._

James M. Reardon
Pastor.

A 1922 diploma signed by
James M. Reardon, Pastor.

"That was a very interesting neighborhood in many ways because, you see, we were right adjacent to the parade grounds, which in those days was the center of all kinds of activities. Every day there must have been eight diamonds of ball games over that whole range of the Parade. And each year there was a big kite flying day when the whole area around there would be filled with hundreds and hundreds of kites. And then across from the parade grounds, near where the Sculpture Garden is now, was the old Armory, an old concrete building. All kinds of things took place there—the Shrine Circus, the Sportsman's Show, the Builder's Show, and the political speeches. I remember going across the parade grounds when I was about ten years old to hear old Bob LaFollette give a speech. The Basilica was not an island or an isolated place at that time; it was in the center of

a remarkably active community."

In 1925, Mr. Connors was a student in a combined fifth and sixth grade class.

"There were two classes in the same room that year, and it must have been very challenging for the nun in charge. You'd have English from a reader, and that was one of the advantages of having two classes going on at the same time. I remember learning all about *The Iliad* and *The Odyssey* while I was supposed to be doing something else. There would be discussion of the literature involved and questions and answers, and then there would be an arithmetic exercise. There would also be the hideous Palmer method of penmanship, with those circles and fences and whatnot. My penmanship grades were wretched.

"And of course we had religion, the Catechism. I remember a delightful occasion in the fifth grade, when the Bible history section of the day was being conducted. My friend Jim was not much of a student. This section of the Bible history was focusing on John the Baptist and his preaching. Sister Adalia was reading from the book how John had told the people 'Trust not to your descent from Abraham. The ax is about to be laid to the root of the tree.' And all at once, noticing that Jim at the back was day-dreaming as usual, she said, 'James, what does that mean?' Well, he tried to bring himself together, and he thought wildly and said, 'That must have been when Abraham Lincoln chopped down the cherry tree!'

"The group of nuns there were generally very capable, I thought. They lived over at St. Margaret's. They would walk over there every day, even in the bitterest winter weather, carrying a big lunch basket for their lunch. They were good teachers. The principal of the parish school during my years there was Sister Grata. (I've learned from Monsignor Reardon's book about the Basilica that her last name was Powers. We never thought of the sisters as having last names.) She was a slightly buxom, red-cheeked genial person, with a good sense of humor, and I'm sure was a capable administrator. I never saw her in an impatient mood. I would judge that the relationship among the teaching sisters at the Basilica was a genuinely congenial one—at least I have never heard happier laughter than that which came from the staff room at lunch time.

"I liked the custom some sisters followed when a fire engine or ambulance siren sounded near the school of having the children say a brief prayer for any victim or victims of the emergency. It has remained a lifelong instant reaction with me, and I suppose with others.

"You'd go out every day for morning and afternoon recess. And at noon you'd come back into the school to a musical accompaniment performed on piano and drums. For two or three years, a charming girl named Marian Madigan pounded the piano and my friend Felix Pepin and I accompanied her on drums. Our regularly performed marching melody was 'Under the Double Eagle,' and I can never hear it without being thrust back seventy years to the middle of the Basilica School's first floor corridor, with schoolmates marching past.

"A memorable feature of my last years in the Basilica School was the formal debates by selected eighth-grade teams, three girls against three boys, before the entire student body. The 1927–1928 topic was, I think, Philippine independence. The topic in the year I debated (1928–1929) was American military intervention in Nicaragua, then going on. Two other boys and I had the affirmative position, and we were soundly trounced by the three girls who argued against the activities of U.S. Marines who were pursuing the insurgent General Sandino. During the 1980s, when

Father Charles Doran, Director of the Altar Boys, stands in the center of his charges.

American intervention in Nicaraguan affairs was a hot issue, I considered writing to President Ronald Reagan that the arguments for American intervention being set forth by his Administration were no more valid than when I was using them unsuccessfully against the Basilica girls when I was fourteen. "

"Father Charles Doran was quite a small man. After the new altar was installed, with its high and deep tabernacle, he had great difficulty reaching into the tabernacle and withdrawing the large monstrance at Benediction services. A small footstool was kept for him on the reverse side of the altar, and an altar boy would bring it out when needed.

"He also stood on a footstool in the pulpit. A story that I believed as a boy but have later decided, with regret, must have been sheer fiction, was that in reading the Gospel one Sunday he accidentally fell off the stool just as he read the Lord's words, 'And a little while and you shall not see me'—and then resurfaced with the words, 'And again a little while, and you shall see me.' That is probably a story that, over the centuries, has been told about every short priest.

"The staff of the Rectory was more like an army headquarters really, with the Command-ing Officer, because there were so many priests. In those early years at the Basilica, there was the pastor, Father Reardon, and at least four assistants. Of course they were very busy and, just as in the Army, there were the regular assignments. They made sick calls, for example. The priest might be called out at any hour of the night.

"They made hospital visits. They went out many times when there was a danger of death and administered what was then called Extreme Unction, the final anointing. There was a complete round of duties and they really needed a large staff.

"One whole summer, maybe it was through a good part of the year, I served Father Reardon's six o'clock Mass, and it was very interesting. He was an aloof kind of person, ordinarily not severe, although he could be. It has rather an interesting pictorial effect in my mind when I look back to those days, coming into that vasty Cathedral when just the altar was lit up, and going into the Sacristy. I'd be there before the six o'clock Mass, of course, and he'd always be kneeling up on a chair, I think probably saying the Rosary. I'd probably say good morning, and he'd say good morning, but it was as if he was on a cloud somewhere. And we wouldn't exchange any conversation at all. I wouldn't even have known whether he knew my name or not except one day I remember, it was on Saint Patrick's Day, his face was wreathed in smiles. And he said, 'Good morning, Joseph.'

"Catholics who have grown up since the abolition of the fasting-from-midnight-before-communion regulation might find it hard to credit how troublesome the regulation was: endless

questions in catechism classes and elsewhere about what did or didn't break the fast, discussions among late-evening restaurant parties about fast or slow watches and time zones—and sometimes genuine physical distress for persons used to early breakfasts, including some altar boys like me. Once, when I was about twelve, having served (fasting) Father Reardon's six o'clock Mass, I was asked by Father Bastyr to serve his seven o'clock Mass, for which the scheduled server hadn't shown up. That was no sooner completed than there appeared in the sacristy an elderly, lanky, grizzled bishop from New Zealand or Australia—a guest and an old friend of Father Reardon's—who wished to say an eight o'clock Mass in the Saint John Vianney chapel, and I was immediately recruited for that service. Fortunately, it was a Saturday rather than a school day, so I was able to stagger home afterwards and recover with a triple order of wheatcakes.

"Father Reardon's sermons were very memorable. They were prepared with great care. And every now and then he'd indulge his passion for American Catholic history with a purely historical sermon—they were very, very good. Sometimes, they were somewhat in the style of the romantic novelist. I remember a sermon of his on the North American martyrs when he began by saying something like 'one day in such and such a year in 16 so-and-so, a dusty world-weary traveller presented himself.' It was just like the beginning of a historical novel. He was a really impassioned amateur historian.

"He was a man born after his time in many respects. He would have been a wonderful frontier missionary, brave and tough, severe upon himself, severe upon others.

"He had, of course, been a protege of John Ireland and was devoted to him, and I think that he modeled himself in many ways on John Ireland. Over the years of studying Ireland and recalling Reardon, I've sometimes been struck by curious coincidences. I remember how Father Reardon himself, with an altar boy situation for example, would sometimes impatiently say

"Nobody really notices the rectory because it's in the shadow of such a stately and magnificent cathedral-type edifice. But were it not for the Basilica, I'm convinced that the rectory would be on historic registers in its own right, and worthy of significant adulation. It's the center of an awful lot of life, a lot of stories, and much history," remarks Father Dennis Dease. The rectory was completed in 1928.

'Good Lord, good Lord!' I'm sure that was Ireland's interjection. I'd heard how Archbishop Ireland had urged people to fast vigorously and adhere to the Lenten fasting regulations which were, of course, very severe. And he'd say, 'You say you'll get a headache? You're supposed to get a headache!' And I remember hearing Monsignor Reardon say precisely that on Ash Wednesday, for as long as I remember.

"His New Year's Day sermon was quite famous. He was, of course, a great temperance man. He'd been one of Ireland's chief apostles in the crusade against the saloon. And I can still hear him saying, 'They say they can take it or leave it alone? Why do they not prove the truth of their declaration by leaving it alone?' That was his style. And he would choose New Year's morning when the pews might have here and there persons with hangovers, to give a really vigorous temperance sermon."

The grand Basilica has always been suited to large-scale events. Here the annual state convention of the Ancient Order of Hibernians gathers on the steps, September 1929.

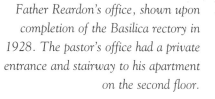

Father Reardon's office, shown upon completion of the Basilica rectory in 1928. The pastor's office had a private entrance and stairway to his apartment on the second floor.

The elements of the Basilica coat of arms, pictured here, read as follows: The Basilica (pavilion or umbrella) of Saint Mary (crescent moon) in the City of Minneapolis (crenelated walls), City of Waters (wavy lines).

On February 1, 1926, the Pro-Cathedral of Saint Mary was raised by the Holy See to the rank of minor Basilica, the first in the United States. Subsequently, it was referred to as the Basilica of Saint Mary. It is said that a "Pro-Cathedral," a church that would someday be replaced by a Cathedral, had never really been an accurate description of the Basilica. It had also led to calling the big church "The Pro," a term that Father Reardon thought "very undignified." The pastor took steps, and "the parishioners rejoiced in the new dignity conferred on their church."

In his history of the Basilica, Monsignor Reardon writes: "Among historic events in the Basilica may be mentioned the memorial service for Marshal Ferdinand Foch, Generalissimo of the allied forces in the first World War [at right]. It was held on Tuesday, March 26, 1929, the very day on which his obsequies took place in Notre Dame Cathedral in Paris.... The Mass was attended by Governor Christiansen, Mayor Leach, Colonel Sweeny of Fort Snelling, and their respective staffs; representatives of the American Legion Posts; Veterans of Foreign Wars; Red Cross Nurses; Boy Scouts; Knights of Columbus and a congregation conservatively estimated at upwards of four thousand persons. Hundreds were unable to obtain admission."

In 1930, a statue honoring the Belgian priest-explorer Father Louis Hennepin, here shown draped, was unveiled in front of the Basilica, on the avenue that bears his name. It was a tremendous civic event—Monsignor Reardon once again reports that "the church was literally packed with people and thousands waited outside during the Mass and sermon brought to them by loud speakers."

Opposite: Father Reardon turns first sod for Father Hennepin Memorial.

The gloriously finished Basilica shone in the thirties as the home of many enormous events, and served as the parish church for a large section of Minneapolis. In 1930, the dedication of a statue of Father Hennepin in its front lawn brought wide recognition to the Basilica and its pastor, who received an award from the King of the Belgians for his efforts. Reardon travelled, leading at least one pilgrimage to Europe and the Holy Land, was a leader in the Knights of Columbus, and welcomed Archbishop Murray for his first pontifical Mass. His writing continued; he finished his history of the Basilica, first published in 1932. The frugality that had enabled him to finish the Basilica's interior in the previous decade continued, as did a kind of private generosity that still survives in small stories.

"One of my fondest memories is of Monsignor Reardon. He used to walk to our house at Christmas time to deliver boxes of candy to us. We lived about one and a half miles from the church. I didn't realize until later that we were poor. He was very good to us and all my brothers served as altar boys because they had loud voices!"

—Parishioner Patricia Cassidy Kyllonen

	AT THE BASILICA	LIFE OF THE CHURCH	CIVIC LIFE
1930	1930 *October 12, Dedication of the Father Hennepin Memorial.* 1932 *January 31, First pontifical Mass, Archbishop Murray.* 1932 *Publication of Monsignor Reardon's history of the Basilica.*	1930 *Archbishop Dowling dies; succeeded by Archbishop John Gregory Murray.*	1930 *Population of Minneapolis is 464,356. Average U.S. income is $1,388 per year. Loaf of bread costs 8.6¢.* 1934 *Teamsters strike in Minneapolis becomes violent.*
1935			1935 *Average U.S. income is $1,115 per year. Loaf of bread costs 5.6¢.*
1940		1939 *Pope Pius XI dies; succeeded by Pope Pius XII.*	1939 *Germany invades Poland; World War II begins.*

A Basilica pilgrimage group is photographed in Rome during the summer of 1930, *"just after it emerged from an audience with Pope Pius XI."* The Pope, Father Reardon recounted, spoke to them for fifteen minutes in Italian, and gave each person a medal. Father Reardon is in the front, to the left of the child. The caption also indicates that his sister and longtime secretary, Miss Agnes Reardon, is present. It was apparently an exciting trip. According to the Minneapolis Star, *the party returned from visits to North*

Africa, Europe and elsewhere "having spent 36 hours in constant peril while their ship nosed its way in a dense fog through a sea of floating icebergs off the coast of Labrador." They had seen the Passion Play in Oberammegau and attended the International Eucharistic Congress in Carthage. Eleven years later, Father Reardon would host a Congress in Minneapolis.

Roland L. Hill, who describes himself as an "internationally recognized expert on 'Where to Go, Stop, Eat, Play and Shop,'" wrote a few notes about the pastor in his cookbook, along with Monsignor Reardon's recipe for broiled liver. "He was gruff and many were afraid of him, but when you knew him he was the kindest and gentlest of men. I always made it a point to go to confession to him because there was never a lineup at his box as most were afraid of him. I was Scoutmaster of Troop 111 at the Basilica for several years and I could always depend on Father Reardon to come through with anything we needed. And when I went up to Duluth to Teachers College during the depression I was flat broke and working for board and room at the YMCA, and lo and behold in the mail came a beautiful Christmas card and a crisp new ten dollar bill in it from Father Reardon. Talk about manna from heaven. I suppose it was the most appreciated and greatest gift I had ever gotten because I was so broke."

The Basilica choir in December 1932, in the sacristy. Father Reardon is center, John Jacob Beck is second to his left and his sister and secretary Agnes Reardon is on his right.

CHOIR BASILICIA OF ST MARYS. DEC 1932.

An undated note in the Basilica archives says that seats were fifteen cents for the seven A.M. mass and twenty-five cents for all other masses.

Seats 15 cents

-46-

Jerry Piazza's family has been in the Basilica parish since the old Immaculate Conception days. The Italian families, he remembers, also included the Grazianos, the Iaconas, the Petris. "In the forties," he remembers, "Joe Petri was there at six o'clock Mass every Sunday and had a little table in front of the church for pew rental. Monsignor Reardon used to collect money for pews, and Mr. Petri was an usher. People drove or walked to church, but a lot of people took the streetcar."

Jerry Piazza tells a good story about the Irish and the Italians at the Basilica. "The old story goes that when I was a little guy in school there—I don't remember what sister it was, she was saying how good the Irish were—most of the nuns were Irish, of course. They went to church every Sunday, they went to confession once a week, went to Communion every Sunday and they were just the best Catholics. So I raised my hand and she said, 'Piazza, what do you want?' And I said, 'Sister, if the Irish are the best Catholics and they do everything right, how come the Pope isn't in Dublin?' And she said, 'Oh, you Italians, you think you can run everything!' I'll never forget that." Was she joking? "Well, I don't know! But I wasn't!" he laughs.

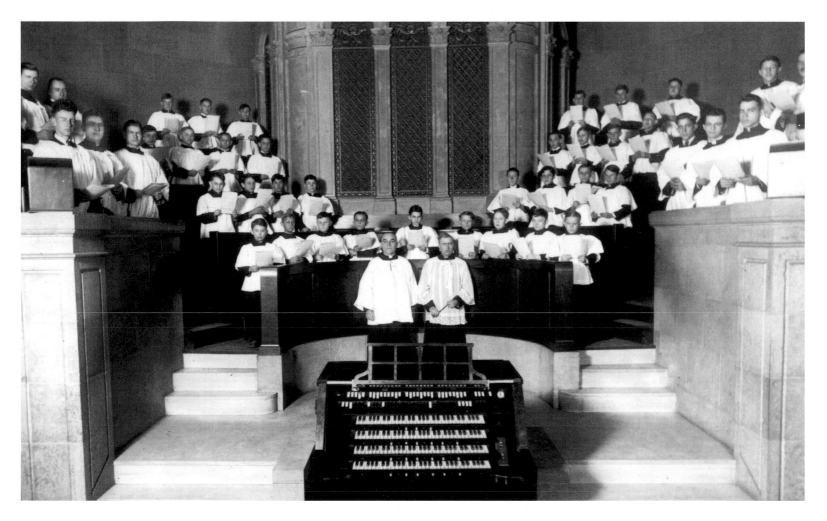

In 1955 Monsignor Reardon wrote that "early in August 1933, John Jacob Beck, organist since 1922, was authorized to organize and train a choir of boys from the upper grades of the Basilica School and its graduates to replace the adult choir of men and women so long a feature of the Sunday services. Since then, the vested boy's choir has sung the responses at the High Masses, chanted the psalms and lamentations during Holy Week, and built up a large and varied repertory of Masses and motets. From time to time the members have broadcasted very acceptably over a national or local hook-up from the Basilica sanctuary and from the studios of the network granting the privilege."

In this 1934 photo, Father Reardon and Professor Beck are front and center in the apse, the vaulted recess behind the high altar.

At center is the Kilgen Orchestral Theater Organ. It is said to have come from a theater in New York City, having been used to accompany the silent movies. Its installation, along with the large organ case seen at the back of this photograph, changed the appearance of that part of the church.

In 1934, Gus Zuccaro was in the seventh grade at the Basilica School, the fifth of twelve children. One morning that spring, he got a surprise.

"It was room 207, I think, and the sister's name was Concordia. I was a kind of a shy type little kid with a reserved personality, and I knew nothing about it. This fellow appears and he announced who he was and they had a special program, and all of a sudden he mentioned my name. Just out of the blue.

Zuccaro was the 1934 winner of a medal presented by the commandant of the American Legion to outstanding seventh grade students at the Basilica. The American Legion school award was for courage, honor, service, leadership, and scholarship.

"It was just a standard way of life for me because my mother was so very straight-laced. My mother walked every day to church and she was just a saint. She'd get back before it was time for us to get up and go to school. We were two miles away, in lower north Minneapolis. There was a small grouping in our neighborhood of about fifteen Italian families. The Piazzas and Cutraras and Famalaros and Natolis and Battaglias and Mandiles and so forth. That's how it was in those early days. If someone came over from the old country, they'd live with friends who helped them along. Dave Piazza and Tony De Lisi and my father and Angelo Battaglia and that group came from the same area in Sicily, and the town they came from was just east of Palermo. And that whole neighborhood belonged to the Basilica.

"All the kids walked together to school. The Italian families stuck together in the parish and we were all kind of proud of the fact that most of us served Mass; there was a kind of camaraderie there.

"Father Reardon had a policy of not having any social

Above right: Gus Zuccaro and schoolboys prepare for a school picnic.

-48-

activities. Baseball, at the extreme insistence of Father Keeler, was the only program at the school that I remember, and it certainly wasn't encouraged. As a result, facilities that normally go along with sports were not there—locker room, equipment, transportation, etc. Our baseball manager was Jack Murray, from a big family of parishioners. Practice and all games were played at the Parade, and everything was after school. We had to wear our uniforms to school and in class all day and after the game would all have to find our way home as on any school day.

"One time we had a game early in the season. It started snowing that day and when school let out there was six to eight inches of snow on the ground. There I was walking home in my baseball uniform in the snow—did I get looked at!"

In the thirties, Father Reardon was in his second decade of leadership at the Basilica. He was ably assisted by his sister and secretary Miss Agnes Reardon, who had been with him since his days as editor-in-chief of the Catholic Bulletin. *In 1936, five-year-old Clarence Birk started in the first grade. Birk is shown here with a holy water font. To the right is the upstairs repository that fed holy water to the first-floor fonts.*

"I came along with my brother who was already a student here. We actually walked the distance from the Second and Penn area, and it was a long walk in the winter. As we came from the west, there were only two large visible structures. One was the Basilica itself and the other was the Foshay Tower. The Basilica still stands out, but, well, the Foshay is no longer a large building!

"Sunday Mass was compulsory. The nine o'clock Mass was the children's Mass, and the nuns always sat with their children in the front; we probably took up the first fifteen rows on each side. Nine o'clock was always full and eleven o'clock was always full. We had a Mass on the hour every hour from six o'clock on.

"The first grade sister at that time was Sister Erminelda. She was, I thought, rather young. She was still here, as a matter of fact, when I graduated in the eighth grade; by then, I could see that she wasn't quite as young as I had thought. Second and third grade was Sister Mary Regis. She was always saying

'Clarence, you're going to be a priest'. But it didn't come about—I married and we have seven children! In eighth grade, Sister Alberta stressed an awful lot how important our grades were. The children who went from Basilica to Catholic high school were expected to be very well trained and ready.

"One of the highlights of the school year was the Coca-Cola company. They did a promotional thing each year, for any children who had five bottle caps. They probably didn't drink the Coke, but they had the caps. The company would come in and they'd give each child a bottle of Coca-Cola, a tablet, a pencil, and a ruler. And that was one of the hot things.

"Another was when the custodian, Adolph Westermeier, would play music. Every year, a few days before the Christmas

holidays, he would make the rounds of every room with his zither, and he would play Christmas melodies for us. He was old, and to me his hands looked awfully big and gnarled. And yet he played some of the most beautiful music with those fingers.

"I think pastors should be given credit for the things they've done. Monsignor Reardon deserves an awful lot of credit for what he did. During one of the worst depressions this country has ever seen, he was able to take the debt of the Basilica and not just reduce it, but completely obliterate it. During the depression, while people were out of jobs!"

Clarence Birk remembers a softer side of Father Reardon, too, who could dress down an altar boy and then slip him some breakfast money.

"As an altar boy, I served the Monsignor on All Soul's Day. On All Soul's Day, at that particular time, he would get onto the altar at seven o'clock and he would say three Masses in a row. Get through with one, start on another one, through the whole Mass again, and he could do a Mass in twenty minutes. He was noted for speed. In rosaries, you had a hard time keeping up. But at any rate, I made a mistake in the third Mass.

"I could tell by the look on his face—and he stopped halfway through that prayer—that this was not going to be good for me at all. And I just dreaded the end of that third Mass. I can feel it to this day, walking back into the sacristy with him behind me. I knew it was coming, and it came. He was very angry. And I'm helping him off with his vestments and he's putting them away and he's wiping out the chalice and he's not letting up on me at all. I don't know if I could have hung my head any lower than that.

"And he got through. And he said, 'Have you had breakfast?' Well, we fasted from midnight on at that time, and I said 'No, Father.' Well, he reached in his pocket and gave me a dollar, and said, 'Go get something to eat!' And that was the kind of priest he was."

The Mass celebrating the consecration of the Basilica's altars on June 27, 1941.

*D*uring World War II, parishioners at the Basilica, as elsewhere, worked, saved, and prayed. The serenity of the building provided a thread of stability to families torn by the war. In his history of the Basilica, Father Reardon reports 653 members of the parish served in the armed forces; twenty-seven died.

The decade began, however, with another of Father Reardon's enormous public enterprises as the diocese hosted the 1941 National Eucharistic Congress. Father Reardon and his pilgrimage group had attended the International Eucharistic Congress in Carthage in 1930; eleven years later, Father Reardon was the general chairman for an event that reportedly involved 450,000 people.

The Basilica was paid off during the forties, thirty-four years after ground was broken; the mortgage was burned during the National Eucharistic Congress. Family life and school life went on, during the War years and after. Father Reardon, now a monsignor and in his third decade of leadership, went on as well.

The front facade of the Basilica was decorated for the Eucharistic Congress.

AT THE BASILICA	LIFE OF THE CHURCH	CIVIC LIFE

1940

1941 *June 9, Father Reardon raised to the rank of monsignor.*

1941 *June, Ninth National Eucharistic Congress.*

1941 *June 27, Consecration of Basilica of Saint Mary altars.*

1940 *Population of Minneapolis is 492,370. Average U.S. income is $1,315 per year. Loaf of bread costs 9.6¢.*

1940 *Minneapolis holds its first Aquatennial Summer Festival.*

1941 *Attack on Pearl Harbor; U.S. joins World War II.*

1945

1945 *Atomic bomb dropped on Japan; end of World War II.*

1945 *Average U.S. income is $2,364 per year.*

1948 *First television station in Minneapolis begins broadcasting.*

1950

The Ninth National Eucharistic Congress, of which Father Reardon was the general chairman, was an enormous project. The Congress was, and still is, one of the conventions of the Roman Catholic Church in America, held every three years. For 1941, the Minneapolis Sunday Tribune reported, "This year, it is more than that. The thirty-fifth international congress was to have been held at Nice, France. War intervened. This week, as across the seas men meet in battle, the army of peace, whose goal is the conquest of the souls of men and women, gathers its forces in this peaceful Land of Lakes."

The Congress received wide coverage in the press. One headline read "Catholic Capital of U.S. moves to Twin Cities." The paper said that "more than one hundred bishops and archbishops were waiting in Minneapolis and Saint Paul. Thousands of priests were here and hundreds of thousands of laymen. Catholic parishes, schools, religious orders and lay organizations from one end of the country to the other were represented. Special trains came rolling into Minneapolis and Saint Paul from almost every state in the union. Busloads of congress pilgrims were coming in a steady procession to bus stations in both cities. State highway patrolmen on all roads leading to the Twin Cities reported incoming traffic at an unprecedented peak. In the two cities, hotels, apartments, rooming houses and private homes were filled to capacity with the congress visitors."

Activities took place all over the Twin Cities. At the Basilica, additional altars were put in, even in the unfinished undercroft, for visiting priests to say their obligatory daily Mass. "All those altars were full of flowers. My cousin Vince and I had the job of going around and filling all the vases with water," remembers Jerry Piazza. He was in third grade at the time.

On June 22, 1941, the Minneapolis Sunday Tribune

A banner from the Eucharistic Congress.

General instructions for the Eucharistic Procession, held on Thursday, June 26, 1941, at 1:30 P.M.

Above right: Marchers at the Eucharistic Congress in 1941.

and Star Journal *included a full-page, full-color photo spread with three photos of Archbishop John Gregory Murray, the official host. The Congress, it reported, would bring together "450,000 members of the Roman Catholic faith." Highlights would be "the opening Pontifical Mass said by the Papal Legate, the Midnight Mass for 100,000 men to be said by the Apostolic Delegate, the Pontifical Mass with a choir of 15,000 children, and the huge Eucharistic Procession, in which more than 50,000 persons will participate." Monday evening's* Minneapolis Daily Times *carried a front page photo of Archbishop Murray across fully half the page. (The head-*

line: "Nazi Lunge Jolts Russ; U.S. Condemns Attack.")

Tuesday, June 24, 1941, there was a full-page photo spread in the Minneapolis Daily Times, *with an aerial shot of crowds gathering for pontifical high Mass at the state Fairgrounds, and a report of ten thousand people "roaring" their welcome to the papal legate at the Minneapolis Auditorium. On the same day, the front page of the* Morning Tribune *carried a photo of the cardinal's arrival with an extended story about the one-hundred-car procession that carried the cardinal from the depot, and another full-page set of photos.*

Thursday's Daily Times *carried two full pages of photos, and*

Amidst the coverage during the week of the Eucharistic Congress was a story about Father Reardon's ascension to monsignor protonotary apostolic. The story reported that he would "wear the robes on the right Friday when eight altars are consecrated at the Basilica in the service especially consecrating that church."

Souvenir of Consecration

"A marble poem, an aesthetic dream of sculptured beauty, fit to be the theme of Angel fancies; a Madonna prayer uttered in stone."

Basilica of St. Mary
Minneapolis, Minnesota
June 27, 1941

Friday's Minneapolis Star Journal *covered the closing, reporting that "rain drenched the jam-packed 125,000 faithful who paid devotion to the Sacred Host at the State fair grounds Thursday in the climaxing act of the Ninth Eucharistic Congress.... No one sought shelter from the storm that came just as the Benediction was closing Thursday's ceremonies at the State fair grounds. Cellophane raincoats shielded the prelates from the rain, yet permitted spectators to view their richly-ornamented ecclesiastic dress. Many knelt in mud to receive the final blessing given them by Cardinal Dougherty."*

The Souvenir of Consecration, from June 27, 1941, lists the presiders for dedicating eight altars and refers to the Basilica as "a marble poem; an aesthetic dream of sculptured beauty, fit to be the theme of Angel fancies; a Madonna prayer uttered in stone." The quote is unattributed.

Choir boys, probably on Palm Sunday, circa 1940. Through the forties, John Jacob Beck continued to lead the Basilica music programs. In 1942, he passed a rigorous examination to become an associate member of the American Guild of Organists. He was the only Catholic in the Minnesota chapter until his death in 1949.

In 1940, the Archbishop authorized daily exposition of the Blessed Sacrament at the Basilica, the first time such permission had been given to any parish in the diocese. The reported purpose was "to honor our Eucharistic Lord, to pray for the restoration and perpetuation of the peace of Christ among individuals and nations," and for the success of the Eucharistic Congress, scheduled for the following year. World War II had engulfed Europe; "hundreds" of parishioners promised to spend a quarter of an hour each week in adoration. An article in the May 4, 1940 Catholic Bulletin reflects on the prayer and peace they found there. Some things about the Basilica never change.

"Some prefer the early morning hours when Masses are being said, when they have companionship in watching, while others select a time when worshippers are few. Among them may be seen children of the parish school who drop in for a brief visit during recess or on the way home, as well as pupils from more distant schools who are less familiar with the sacred place; men and women on their way to and from work; clerks from stores and offices during the noon hour; housewives in the afternoon; laborers in working clothes; business and professional men; tourists and visitors on sightseeing trips. All are animated by the same purpose—to pay tribute to the Son of God beneath the sacramental veils.

"Within the Basilica with its towering grandeur, its massive dome, its vaulted nave, there is an atmosphere of the supernatural, quiet and restful. The hurry and bustle of the encircling city with its myriad interests and throbbing life cease at the threshold. Inside peace and serenity reign. Even a whisper breaks the silence that is eloquent of the world of spirit. An unseen Presence broods over all and prayer is the voice of the soul. One is on holy ground."

In the summer of 1940, the Minneapolis Red Cross unit of the Archdiocesan Council of Catholic Women met weekly to do "war work," making clothing to be sent to war-torn Europe. Seventy-six women, twenty-one of whom did knitting at home, participated, representing the Catholic parishes of the city and meeting in the same room that had been used for the same purpose during World War I. They met all day Tuesdays, using six sewing machines to produce women's dresses, children's pinafores, shawls, sweaters, and blankets.

The work expanded in following years to include chapters in other parishes and continued through the end of the war. The numerically minded Monsignor Reardon gives yearly totals of hours worked and garments produced, and always breaks out the work of Basilica women. The totals are astonishing: thousands of workers, tens of thousands of garments, and hundreds of thousands of surgical dressings.

Roselyn De Lisi Glenn was a student during the late forties and fifties. Her mother's family belonged to the Immaculate Conception parish before 1900.

"I can remember at Basilica School sitting on the merry-go-round reading fortunes and singing songs. The hard pavement on the playground led to many injured knees. There was no gym in the school. On Fridays for lunch, there was tomato soup, sandwiches and pudding. We all sang in the choir on holy days, attended Mass on first Fridays and ended each week with Benediction. Everyone remembers the high Masses, smell of incense, bishops' visits and the Blessed Sacrament in the tabernacle being exposed continually. In the morning, we marched into school to the record by Sousa's band. We are all grateful to our families for our religious foundation and to the Basilica Church for being such a steady instrument."

Another school memory from the forties, this one from Susan Erlougher Sicora.

"I became a student at the Basilica School in the fourth grade and remember well, with a certain amount of dread, the appearance of the Right Reverend Monsignor Reardon in the classrooms on report card day. He would appear at the desk in the front of the room, and read off all the students' grades to the whole class. I recall it was with great speed he did this, so no one really remembered anyone's grades but their own, but it was intimidating nevertheless. Another fond (?) remembrance is of Confession Day. Monsignor Reardon had a very loud voice and most of us spent the waiting-in-line time covering our ears trying not to hear any remarks he made regarding others' venial, or more likely mortal, sins emanating from the confessional. I vividly remember hoping to end up in the line for Father Quinlan's confessional instead."

Confessional marked with priest's name.

Mrs. Anne Lahiff Klein, center, and her two sisters, Mary Elizabeth (Mel) Lahiff and Eileen Lahiff Grundman, are members of a family who have been members of the Basilica and its predecessor parish since 1867. Since 1919, they say, "all their family events" have taken place at the Basilica.

Above: This photo is simply marked "1947. Sister Bernard. Sister Albertus. 8th Grade Guys."

"My aunts Elizabeth and Annie Quinlan, when this building was built, gave the Sacred Heart altar in honor of their sister who had recently died. And all these outdoor railings are Aunt Annie's; she gave them because she didn't like walking up and down the stairs without something to hold on to. They were good friends of Monsignor Reardon, our aunts Annie and Elizabeth Quinlan.

"But the best memories, I think, are the teachers and the respect that we had for them, and in particular our eighth grade sister, Sister Albertus. She respected us and we respected her. It was sort of a two-way street. I think everyone there just thought she was so great. She told us in the eighth grade that we were old enough to see adult-aged movies. Of course, that made us feel pretty big! And during recess one day, she brought out the wind-up Victrola. We all brought records and we danced during recess instead of going outside, because she figured we should learn. That was the kind of thing we ought to be doing."

During the second World War, as of November 1, 1945, the parish was represented in the armed forces by 653 people, including thirty-three women and three chaplains. Twenty-seven "made the supreme sacrifice," dying in North Africa, the Philippine Islands, Italy, Germany, the South Pacific, in hospital, or simply "at sea." At home, many had watched and waited.

"In 1942, I got married at the Basilica. When war was declared, I moved back home. I got a job a couple of blocks from the church, and went to Mass every morning, for my husband's safety in the Pacific. Home without a scratch."

—Mrs. Marguerite Greene

"It was a cold and windy day on November 16, 1946 when Henry and I were married at the Basilica of Saint Mary. In August, V. J. Day had ended the long and painful World War II. Many of us awaited the return of family and sweethearts, and our hearts ached for those who did not return. Throughout our country, thousands of couples were being married 'after the war.'

"There were many couples being married at the Basilica. There were no afternoon or evening weddings, only Saturday morning. The time slots were 7, 8, 9 and 10 A.M. We were given 8 A.M. by Monsignor Reardon. The fact that our families had to drive in from the country was irrelevant. Hank's family got up before dawn, milked the cows, did the chores and drove over one hundred miles and were at the Basilica before 8 A.M.—and there were no freeways! Hank and his brother, Ira, wore their uniforms. My sister Audrey and I wore suits and large black hats. At that time, there were no pictures taken in the church. There were several snapshots taken on the steps of the Basilica.

"We have seven children and eight grandchildren, and are a three generation family at the Basilica. In 1996, we celebrated our fiftieth anniversary with a beautiful Mass."

—Kathleen Baron

Altar boy Jerry Piazza and friends at the Basilica, 1945.

Longtime parishioner Jerry Piazza remembers being an altar boy at the Basilica in the forties.

"You had to first be a torchbearer. Then you had to learn the Latin prayers. There was an altar boy priest, and you had to recite them for him. Then you got to be an acolyte and you usually served Mass with an older altar boy. When we recited the prayers at the foot of the altar like we used to, Monsignor Reardon said, 'You have to be heard all the way in the back of the church.' So you had to say them very loud! We had a lot of altar boys, two for every Mass. You had to be there a half-hour early. Then we had Benediction during the week, and you had to bring your rosary with you. Monsignor Reardon would say, 'Boys, do you have your beads?' If you didn't have your beads, you had to stay in back of the altar. You couldn't go around in the front."

Scaffolding filled the nave for repair of the ceiling in 1952.

*T*he tireless Monsignor Reardon, now in his eighties, undertook still more building work, redecorating the interior in the colors of Mary, installing bronze doors, even sandblasting the exterior and treating it with a pigeon repellant. In 1955, he completed the revision of his seminal book The Basilica of Saint Mary of Minneapolis, *after having published an exhaustive history of the Diocese of Saint Paul in 1952. People remember he was always working and writing; his highly detailed work now provides base documentation of the early beginnings of the diocese · and the Basilica. In his foreword to the diocesan history, the archbishop refers to Monsignor Reardon's "three years of toil in widespread research." In the twenty-first century, we are the beneficiaries of those many hours spent at his desk. The manuscript, Monsignor Reardon notes, was typed by his sister Agnes. Miss Reardon, a powerful figure in the parish, was his secretary for sixty years.*

He had other help. The life of a parish is labor-intensive, centered on its people, its families and old folks, and on the steady rhythm of baptisms, weddings and funerals that punctuate the years. There are pastoral visits, counseling, sacraments—people work as well as administrative work. Monsignor Reardon had always had a corps of young priests as assistants, living in the rectory under his stern eye and carrying out the work in his way.

Ceiling work in 1952. A bid letter from the Saint Paul Statuary Company, "ecclesiastical designers, sculptors and decorators," specifies painting of the nave, gallery and arches, ambulatories, vestibule, the ceiling of the sanctuary domes, the ceiling of the choir and ambulatory and the sacristy ceiling. Cleaning of marble work, statues and altars is designated.

The Basilica's application to the National Register of Historic Places includes this description of the ceiling work in the fifties.

"In 1953 the interior of the Basilica was redecorated at a cost of $40,000, restoring the original color scheme. The colors used are those of the Virgin Mary as stated in the doctrines of the church. These are: white for purity, blue for truth, red for love, and gold for glory. All ornament is highlighted by the application of gold leaf. Sculptured and molded figures and cartouches throughout the church have been executed and highlighted according to the aforementioned scheme."

-63-

The eighth grade graduating class of 1957, with Monsignor Reardon at center. Father Martin Fleming is on the right.

AT THE BASILICA	LIFE OF THE CHURCH	CIVIC LIFE

1950

1950   *October 15, Dedication concert of Wicks organ.*

1950   *Population of Minneapolis is 521,718.*
       Average U.S. income is $3,180 per year.
       Pound of bread costs 15.3¢.
1950   *Korean War breaks out.*

1953   *Ceiling redecorated.*
1954   *Bronze doors installed.*

1955

1955   *Exterior sandblasted.*
1955   *Publication of Monsignor Reardon's updated*
       history of the Basilica.

1956   *Archbishop Murray dies; succeeded by*
       Archbishop William Brady.
1958   *Pope Pius XII dies; succeeded by Pope John XXIII.*
1958   *Archdiocese of St. Paul becomes*
       Archdiocese of St. Paul and Minneapolis.

1955   *Average U.S. income is $4,128 per year.*
       Pound of bread costs 19.1¢.

1960

Conversation with Father Martin Fleming is laced with laughter, memories, and just a bit of an Irish turn of speech. Fleming grew up in St. Paul and has two older brothers who are priests. The seminary is a difficult course of study and on Christmas of 1951, he was looking forward to his ordination and a different schedule.

"Well, I was getting tired of the seminary, having to go back at 4:15 even on days off, and so on, and I was telling my brothers that next Christmas I'm not going to have to go back at all. And one of them laughed and said, 'Who knows? You may be at the Basilica of Saint Mary and then you won't get off at all. You'll have duty!' Well, then at ordination, my oldest brother John was my chaplain. He opened my letter of appointment, which was handed to us in the Sanctuary, and he said, 'Martin, it's true! You're going to the Basilica!' And sure enough, the next Christmas, the Christmas of 1952, I was on duty here and I didn't get home at all.

"I was here from June of 1952 to June of 1958 as an associate pastor. When I first came, I was the fifth assistant, because there was a priest kind of hovering in place, waiting to enter military service. And then it was four, and then it was three. By the time I left there were just three assistants here in addition to the pastor.

"Monsignor Reardon went through assistants like Kleenex! He was a charming old guy, well up in years, but a real character. We made our own community. There was camaraderie in the household; we protected each other and so on. And you know, it was good work, and we were enthusiastic priests.

"The way he kept track of the assistants was that each of you could be gone one meal a week, and you had to be here for the rest of it. On the second floor of the rectory, there's a place on the step that's a little worn—I imagine it's still there. Well, Reardon used to come out at five minutes before the meal time and he would stand there, and he would put his foot on the step. And then at exactly noon or six o'clock, he would run up the

This crucifix bears the names of the eighth grade class of 1954.

Above right: From the west, 1958.

stairs and go to his place at the table, and there was a little thing under the rug that he would press. Then the doors would swing open and his food would come.

"Reardon would eat very fast. The stuff would be piping hot, and there would be tears coming down our eyes as we tried to keep up with him.

"He was quite deaf, and he was not long on patience. We had these conversations at table, part of which he could hear, and part of which he couldn't hear. It was our chore to keep the humor of the part he could hear connected with the part he couldn't hear, so he wouldn't necessarily know what we were laughing at.

"He had a traditional Irish sense of humor, and a lot of color and character. He was writing his book at the time and he would have dinners which would have these very formal toasts, and he

would write them down. One of his friends was Monsignor Dunphy, whose sister, Sister Bernard Dunphy, was the principal of our school for many years. He would make the assistants come, so we could witness his glory. And every once in a while, Dunphy, who wasn't very demonstrative, would go like this."

Here, Fleming waves his hand dismissively in the air.

"Dunphy was famous for this gesture; he would go like this and say, 'Aaah, shut up, Jim!' We would be stuffing napkins in our faces to keep from laughing.

"I was very fond of Monsignor Reardon. He believed what he believed. He was brought up in a different church. He ran the Eucharistic Congress. He got this church consecrated and declared a basilica. He put those bronze doors on; he finished the interior. He was fiercely confrontive. And he got all that out of the nickels and dimes, as he said many times. It wasn't from

Part of the vested boy choir singing carols on Christmas Day, 1953.

the carriage trade. Monsignor Reardon was not pastorally inclined; in our terms he was an old church administrator.

"There was no effort to reach out to the people. There were no organizations, no men's group, no women's group, no outreach—it just wasn't thought of. It was pay, pray and obey.

"The people came in large numbers because it was their parish church, and the parish was enormous. The nine, ten, eleven, and probably twelve o'clock Masses were full. The rest of them were not standing room only, but they would be full.

"Reardon had a marvelous humor. He would go over to the school and he would pose in his Monsignor's outfit for the group picture with the eighth graders, and he'd get his individual picture taken free. He never wasted anything. When he'd had cancer and was having some treatments, he looked awful. He gave us all eight by ten pictures of himself and wrote on them in

Latin. I can't remember the Latin, but I can remember the English. It's the story from the Scriptures where the apostles are scared when Jesus is walking on the water and the storm is going on; they think he's a ghost. And so Reardon, looking very much like a ghost, just terrible, wrote in Latin on this picture, 'Fear not! It is I!'

"He was able to laugh at death and look it right in the face. He had a mighty faith, he really and truly did."

In 1950, a grand new organ was installed and dedicated at the Basilica, having been ordered the year before, before the death of John Jacob Beck. Charles Hendrickson of the Hendrickson Organ Company makes the point "that the big 1950 dedicatory event at the Basilica was a very rare example of a public 'concert' in either the Basilica or the Cathedral of Saint Paul. Until the 1970s, it was 'Mass only' in these places. Concerts, recitals, and other programs simply were not done." The concert was broadcast and televised live by KSTP-TV. The Diapason, a professional journal, published a front page story on the new organ and noted that "in connection with the dedication, members of the Minnesota Chapter of the American Guild of Organists dedicated a plaque to the late John Jacob Beck, for twenty-seven years director of the Basilica choir. Until his death a year ago, he led the only Catholic boy choir in the diocese."

Dr. Kim Kasling, the Basilica's organist from 1981 to the present day, plays the Wicks organ. "When I first came here and saw that the organ had been built by the Wicks Company, I thought 'ho hum.' They had built thousands of small, rather undistinguished instruments. And then I played it for my audition and said 'Well, this is extraordinary!' I'd never heard an old Wicks that sounded like that, or had those resources. Later on, I checked with the company and got into some of the records and found out that a good part of it had been designed by Henry Vincent Willis IV of England, who had designed the world's largest organ at Atlantic City. That's the reason it has the extraordinary sound it does."

Passion Sunday in 1951: more than 1,200 Knights of Columbus and their families and friends attending. The Knights of the Nicollet General Assembly provided an honor guard. Because of heavy snowfall that morning the grand march to the Radisson Hotel was cancelled.

The piers of Interstate 94 rise next to the Basilica in the mid-sixties.

*A*t the same time that it provides spiritual continuity, a church also reflects the life of its times. Some of the same turbulent flavors that changed the world outside touched the Basilica in the sixties, and the work of the Second Vatican Council profoundly affected the church. From 1962 to 1965, church leaders gathered annually in Rome in a council that became the symbol of the church's openness to the modern world. From the Basilica, Bishop Leonard Cowley attended all four sessions.

At the Basilica, the pace of change was swift, beginning with the death of Monsignor Reardon in 1963. The freeways came, razing the neighborhood and changing the parish and the community forever. The size of the parish was reduced. The Basilica was finally invited to join the Protestants of Minneapolis in their ecumenical Thanksgiving service. The building itself was lightened and brightened by Monsignor Reardon's successor, Bishop Cowley. And the Sisters of Saint Joseph, who had cherished the parish's children for so many years, went in less than one decade from habits to the possibility of bubble hairdos.

Bruce Larsen directs the Schola and orchestra from the choir stalls.

AT THE BASILICA	LIFE OF THE CHURCH	CIVIC LIFE

1960

AT THE BASILICA	LIFE OF THE CHURCH	CIVIC LIFE
1960s *Freeways surround Basilica and split its neighborhood.*	1961 *Archbishop Brady dies; succeeded by Archbishop Leo Binz.*	1960 *Population of Minneapolis is 482,872. Average U.S. income is $4,816 per year. Pound of bread costs 22.8¢.*
	1962 *Second Vatican Council opens in Rome.*	1961 *Twins and Vikings play first major-league seasons in Minnesota.*
1963 *December 13, Monsignor Reardon dies at age ninety-one. Bishop Leonard P. Cowley becomes pastor.*	1963 *Pope John XXIII dies; succeeded by Pope Paul VI.*	1963 *Assassination of President John F. Kennedy.*
		1963 *Tyrone Guthrie Theater opens.*

1965

AT THE BASILICA	LIFE OF THE CHURCH	CIVIC LIFE
		1964 *U.S. involvement in Vietnam War deepens.*
1965 *New Basilica convent ready for occupancy.*		
1966 *Basilica is dedicated as co-cathedral of the Archdiocese of St. Paul and Minneapolis.*	1967 *Leo C. Byrne becomes Coadjutor Archbishop.*	
		1968 *Assassinations of Senator Robert Kennedy and Martin Luther King, Jr.*

1970

In December of 1963, during his customary afternoon prayers in the Basilica, with a rosary in his hand, Monsignor Reardon died at the age of ninety-one. His long and active life had continued right until the end. He had celebrated early morning Mass that morning, and only a few weeks before had conducted a requiem high Mass for assassinated President John F. Kennedy—he had been a priest for seventeen years when Kennedy was born. Monsignor Reardon was the last remaining priest in the Twin Cities to have been ordained by Archbishop John Ireland; his longtime friend Monsignor John Dunphy had died a month earlier, and Monsignor Reardon preached the eulogy. His sister Agnes had left her secretarial duties because of illness, and she would pass away the following year. An editorial said, "Monsignor James M. Reardon and the Basilica of Saint Mary seemed almost synonomous. He died as he lived much of his life—at prayer. Yet a great deal more was crowded into his sixty-five years of priesthood: teacher, editor of the archdiocesan paper, orator, administrator. He was a man of precise habits, a strict disciplinarian with himself and those who served under him. Above all, perhaps, he was deeply respected. An associate termed him the 'last of the clerical gentlemen. He was a fine link with the past, a tradition himself, a devoted servant of his church.'" Still, the church was changing. The Office of the Dead, usually said in Latin, was read in English for the first time at the Basilica at Monsignor Reardon's funeral.

In December of 1963, Bishop Leonard P. Cowley became the pastor of the Basilica. Cowley was born, educated, and ordained in St. Paul. He had been the pastor of St. Olaf in Minneapolis and had served as the administrator and Vicar General of the Archdiocese. Father Alfred Wagner remembers him as "a very talented man with tremendous speaking ability. He would just regale people with stories and bon mots." Father Michael O'Connell said, "I think Bishop Cowley brought a new style of pastoring. He brought his congenial nature. He was very smart and humorous and he was the first segue away from Monsignor Reardon. He linked up with the neighboring pastors; he was well-known and well-liked." He was also an outspoken foe of bigotry and prejudice.

Above right: The new lighting fixtures installed in the Basilica, circa 1965. They were eventually referred to, without affection, as the "spider lights."

A letter from Bishop Cowley details the work he initiated on the parish buildings after his arrival.

"When I became the pastor of Basilica parish, I was happy to assume the responsibilities, and I am still very proud of my job. Poor Monsignor Reardon, my predecessor, had amassed over $1,000,000 in the parish treasury. He was old and tired and had not met some of the exigencies of the parish to the parishioners' satisfaction. Yet he had gathered the funds for this to be done. Accordingly, I set about, as soon as I arrived, to do what I judged had to be done."

The improvements were massive. In the church, all new wiring, new lighting fixtures, new vestments and "altar appurtenances," repairs on the organ and stone work for the sanctuary and baptistry. In the school, new wiring, refinishing the basement, rebuilding of offices and toilets, new lighting fixtures and cabinets, a new library and choir room, new furniture, and painting and decorating of the whole school. In the rectory, new wiring, new windows, new kitchen, new carpeting and furniture and more. There was landscaping of the area, blacktopping and a new school fence.

And there was a new convent. The teaching sisters moved in at Christmastime of 1966.

Bishop Cowley reported $909,000 spent on capital improvements.

The three choirs together on the Basilica steps with Bruce Larsen.

Musically, the 1960s were a particularly brilliant era at the Basilica, as Dr. Kim Kasling relates.

"Bruce Larsen was here, I believe, from 1964 to 1968, as Director of Music and Liturgy with a men's choir, a women's choir that was called the Angelicum, and a boy's choir. That was a brilliant era. There were three pipe organs in the Basilica at the time, and one of the best known composers of church music alive today in the United States, Richard Proulx, was heavily involved. Larsen brought two small pipe organs of his own in. There was one perched up in the choir loft in the gallery at the back, and he had another one down on the floor on the ambulatory column right across from the pulpit. Those were built in Germany. There must have been a lot of chirping going on in that period, and a lot of whistling. He was an extraordinarily gifted musician."

Larsen moved to the Basilica from St. Olaf's upon request of the newly-appointed Bishop Cowley. Mr. Larsen, it is said, led a life devoted to music. He researched, collected, performed, wrote, and directed the gamut of musical works. A sample of his programming, from the bulletin of March 1966: "On Easter Sunday, the 'Great Mass' of Charles Widor, written for two choirs, two organs and orchestra, has been selected for the 11 A.M. high Mass. A guest choir composed of Scholastics from the Jesuit College in Mound will take one of the choir parts, singing from the sanctuary. The three Basilica choirs will be combined to form the second choir. Orchestra music and accompaniment will be by members of the Minneapolis Symphony."

By pride of place, by size and by designation from the archdiocese, the Basilica always held a position of leadership in the religious community of Minneapolis. In the 1960s, it was practicing ecumenical outreach. One of its active partners in that effort was Rabbi Max A. Shapiro, at that time the Senior Rabbi of Temple Israel.

"In 1947, five Protestant churches, Plymouth Congregational Church, Hennepin Avenue United Methodist Church, Westminster Presbyterian Church, the Cathedral Church of St. Mark (Episcopal) and Wesley United Methodist Church, came together for an annual Thanksgiving service. I was friendly with their clergy, and when I became Senior Rabbi of Temple Israel in 1963, I suggested that the two other downtown congregations, the Basilica and Temple Israel, join them. In 1977, the First Christian Church was added to our union."

Getting to know each other was not always easy.

"When Archbishop Leo Byrne came to the Twin Cities, Bishop Cowley invited the Minneapolis clergy to a luncheon of welcome. I was seated to the right of the Archbishop. It was a Friday and, in deference to the Archbishop, I ordered fish, and I don't even like fish."

Rabbi Shapiro also participated in the early days of the Downtown Pastors Association.

"The Downtown Pastors Association was the idea of Dr. Howard Conn of Plymouth Congregational. We came together primarily to learn to know each other better, and to talk about problems that we faced as clergy. Thereafter it was easy to call upon one another when common concerns occurred."

Father Michael O'Connell, still active in that organization, looks back.

"In 1968 there was so much civil unrest—Dr. Martin Luther King, Jr. was assassinated, Robert Kennedy, the Democratic convention. And two years before that, Minneapolis had its own urban violence up on Plymouth Avenue. All of that became overwhelming for the infrastructure of the city. Rabbi Shapiro, Bishop Cowley, and the leaders of St. Mark's Cathedral and Plymouth Congregational got together to see if there wasn't some moral force that they could bring to the discussion. That was the origin of the Downtown Pastors Association, which is still extremely strong today.

"A lot of us had grown up in a fairly prejudicial environment when it came to interfaith efforts, in the fifties. Then when Vatican II happened, we had to do a turnaround. The highest level of teaching of the Roman Catholic Church said, essentially, that these other faiths have validity in and of themselves. They have religious integrity. Rather than going out and trying to convert them, we'll go out and try to understand them. And in doing that, we'll create a much better world of peace and tolerance. Any time you dispel ignorance, you open up the possibility for a relationship and trust. As a matter of fact, you're going to learn a whole lot more about your own faith in that dialogue."

Mary Clare Korb, CSJ, is shown at left near the front pew once reserved for the Sisters of St. Joseph of Carondelet. A card identifying the pew for the sisters is still in place. Some things remain the same over time. Many people remember the teachers of the Basilica School with affection and respect. In the sixties, Sister Mary Clare Korb taught second grade, along with her fellow members of the Sisters of St. Joseph of Carondelet.

Some of the Basilica "footballers" in September 1968.

"I started in the 1962–63 school year and ended with the 1970–71 school year. We had one classroom of every grade, second grade through eighth. There was not a first grade at the time because the pastor, Monsignor Reardon, believed that his school should be staffed by all sisters, and no lay teachers. So when the sister who was there before I came, in first grade, got sick and died, he closed the first grade room.

"I taught the lowest grade, the second grade. Sister Barbara was in third grade. Fourth grade was Sister Rosemarie, and fifth grade was Sister Rose Cecily, sixth grade was Sister Emma Joseph. Seventh grade was Sister Anton and eighth grade was Sister

Georgetta and she was a teaching principal. She had her eighth grade room right across from the office where the telephone was located and her students would go out and answer the phone.

"What was interesting, though, about being at Basilica and what I really loved about it was the variety of people in that school. The children came from five neighborhoods. There was the North Project, which was a building project just north of Basilica, where the Munsingwear was. Then we had the Bryn Mawr area, and then there was Kenwood, Lake of the Isles, and then the downtown section. They came from such different cultures and economic backgrounds. We had the very richest and the very poorest and such a variety was wonderful for the school. There was a wonderful spirit with the children; they were very

respectful of each other.

"The children were encouraged to attend eight o'clock Mass every morning, and the sisters took turns watching the students and bringing them over to the school afterwards. From third grade up, they all received communion and had fasted since the night before.

"The children would go down to the basement where there were these bakery rolls, not healthy at all, and they'd have a carton of milk and they'd sit down very quiet at the tables and eat their breakfasts. I loved it when they were all outside playing on the playground after breakfast. At the sound of the big bell on the outside of the school, everyone would stop the game and stand still. Sister Anton would come out and she'd blow a

1963

1969

1970

whistle and she said, 'Now everyone pick up some paper on the playground on your way to the lines.' And they all picked up some paper, dropped it in the basket and everyone went in silence to their classrooms, and sat down to begin the day.

"The sisters lived at Saint Margaret's Academy and traveled back and forth by a regularly-scheduled Yellow Cab.

"In the morning, it was terrible because sometimes they couldn't find us at Saint Margaret's. They always had a different driver and some days we would stand in the doorway watching for the cab and the younger always got the job of running out there to wave them down. And then we'd get in the cab. There were seven of us, so we were four in the wide seat in the back. They had two little jump seats between the driver, and the principal Sister Georgetta sat in front. Once in a while she would get in a conversation with a cab driver and he would tell us real funny stories. Monsignor had it all worked out so it was a flat rate, and we had the best buy.

"When Bishop Cowley came on, he didn't want us to have to cab, so we had a rental car from the Pontiac garage down there on Hennepin, a station wagon. And he told Georgetta that he wanted us to get our drivers' licenses and have a little more freedom for going back and forth."

In Sister Mary Clare's nine years at the Basilica, the pastors changed, and enormous improvements were made to the facility, including a new convent. The neighborhood around the Basilica was destroyed as the highway came in. And the habit went away. Looking at the pictures, she laughs.

"This is the way I looked when I came and this is the way I looked when I left. The middle one is kind of a transition time. We were able to wear colors and I probably wore this gray because I was so tired of black, black, black. Then finally we got to wear colors and that was really nice. This dress was red, and my sister did my hair. And that's what the Basilica people went through in seeing us! One day after we didn't wear the long black habit anymore, one of the little children went home and his mother said, 'Well, how did your teacher look?' And he said, 'She has legs and high heels on!' Well, I never wore high heels, but he thought they were!"

In 1966, the Basilica of Saint Mary was named by Archbishop Leo Binz as Co-Cathedral of the Archdiocese of Saint Paul and Minneapolis. The archbishop became the official pastor; the priest in charge of the parish would henceforth be known as the rector.

Two active parishioners who were moving out of the area provided this overview to the parish newsletter in July 1966. Its themes are still familiar today.

"The Basilica is a very unusual parish. It is unlike the typical suburban parish with people of like age, economic abilities, educational background, and common interests forged by similar experiences, where any one small group probably represents the views of the majority. It isn't even a typical city parish comprised of one ethnic or social group. The Basilica Parish boundaries circumscribe a heterogeneous collection of people whose economic, social, ethnic, educational and political interests are varying, and whose parish needs are often competing. We are different, and our approach to parish life must reflect this fact.

"The Basilica is an intriguing conglomeration of the past and the future, beauty and ugliness, pathos and promise, young and old, wealth and poverty, decay and rejuvenation. To tackle the problems of the Basilica is to sample the problems facing modern American—education, poverty, racial integration, core city decay and renovation and a faceless, ever-changing population. But more importantly, it is to attempt a synthesis of the Church's role in these areas and to establish, by trial and error, pertinent and viable programs.

"Participation in parish activities quickly brings one face to face with these problems. Opinions were, and are, strongly held and articulated. Positions taken in the past are firmly defended in the present. Interests are varied and seem irreconcilable. Competition for our limited funds can be intense. Yet deep underneath, a common bond to the welfare of the parish is apparent and mediates the differences as required. In order to function, the Basilica must be a forum of compromise, a trading place of this interest for that, and yet it must also honor the diversity of its members so as to serve their individual needs. "

By 1966, although Bishop Cowley was recuperating from an illness, many parish activities were up and active. An unscientific sampling of the New Life, a newsletter that was in its second volume in that year, reveals the existence of a Basilica lecture series, Hospitality Sundays (when parishioners breakfasted in each other's homes), and a very active Home and School Association, with chairs for cultural enrichment, athletic, and ballet, and a Parish Social Service Committee. The Friends of the Library were having teas, the Schools of Religion were sponsoring speakers, and the Young Adults held events and elections. Their column was entitled "Where the Action Is."

There were Parish Parties, and the first annual Parish Picnic; "some 350 people enjoyed charcoal-broiled hotdogs prepared by the Basilica Boy Scouts." The Basilica Athletic Association held an awards dinner and awarded athletic letters and pins to one hundred and twenty-nine boys and girls.

The first Parish Meeting was held on December 7, 1967. Its stated purposes were

- to conform with the intent of Vatican II in implementing the help of the laity in parochial affairs;
- to lay the groundwork for a parish council in the near future;
- to begin in outlining work that the laity in the parish might take on as a community; and
- to establish good communications between our priests and people.

The sixties were a time of change at the Basilica. The biggest physical change was the coming of the freeways. The neighborhood immediately to the west came down, and later just to the north. Father Michael O'Connell, who would beome rector in 1991, looks back.

"The story essentially started with the Eisenhower administration and the interstate highway system. Sometime around 1959 or '60, the federal government people started to inform the various cities where they wanted to lay out these highways, and there were meetings all over the country. The various entities that were going to be affected showed up at these meetings.

"There was a series of meetings here that involved Hennepin Avenue Methodist Church, St. Mark's, the North American Life Insurance Company, and the Basilica, and perhaps some others. The pastors were all there and the various executives and so on. Essentially, the government people said, 'Well, here's where it's going to go.' Monsignor Reardon was here at the Basilica. And he was ninety years old. And the story is that he got up at the meeting and announced that he forbade that from happening, and then he walked out.

"It might be an apocryphal story, but it wouldn't have been unlike him. Consultation was not his strong point. Had he been younger and more amenable to working with groups, the outcome might have been different. The ones that stayed at the table succeeded in getting part of the roadway tunnelled. But the tunnel ends before it gets to the Basilica.

"When the road came through, it started a whole lot of

Interstate 94 tunnel construction, 1965.

events in this parish. It stripped out a very important contiguous neighborhood of homes. Then Highway 394 came in on the north and the parish was imprisoned. It became an island, with no residential community immediately around it. The neighborhood just east of us became a very unsavory place. Loring Park had a bad reputation. I don't think it's true that the road is the primary culprit in terms of the structural insecurity of the Basilica church. Probably the worst effect it's had is in the carbon dioxide emissions in the air; the buildings have just been eaten up.

"But, it was a good news/bad news situation. It took out the housing, isolated the neighborhood. Any feeling of immediate intimate neighborhood disappeared, and there were vibrations and emissions and all that. But I finally figured out that it's actually a wonderful opportunity because now it gives the Basilica huge visibility and accessibility. There's no way we could be doing the things we're doing in the nineties without that."

Pro. Cathedral, Minneapolis, Minn.

M-53—BASILICA OF ST. MARY, MINNEAPOLIS, MINN.

NEW PRO-CATHEDRAL. MINNEAPOLIS. MINN.

146:—Basilica of St. Mary, Minneapolis, Minn.

*T*he Basilica of Saint Mary, now a co-cathedral with the Cathedral of Saint Paul, had always had a history of interest in its neighborhood and community, but the seventies saw a blooming of outreach programs that began a new phase of work for social justice. Programs begun in the seventies would grow for decades and, in some cases, the same parishioners would labor for years to feed the needy and care for the community.

The Basilica School, faced with declining enrollment, closed in the spring of 1975, its remaining students scattered among other parochial and public schools.

In that same year, the church was named to the National Register of Historic Places, ratifying a designation less formally recognized for decades by the region. And it was always filled with music, this decade with a new and daring innovation —the guitar mass!

At far left is the earliest Basilica post card, a watercolor by Emmanuel Masqueray; many other versions followed over the years. Mostly undated, they show different street and entrance configurations, but the majesty of the building is always at center. In 1975, the Basilica's historic and architectural importance was recognized by its inclusion on the National Register of Historic Places.

1680-1930

a of St. Mary

Photo by D. J. Nordgren

The Basilica School in October 1974, the last year of operation.

AT THE BASILICA	LIFE OF THE CHURCH	CIVIC LIFE

1970

1971 *Parish Council formed.*

1972 *Monsignor Terrance Berntson becomes rector.*

1970 *Population of Minneapolis is 434,400.
Average U.S. income is $7,679 per year.
Pound of bread costs 28.5¢.*

1972 *IDS Center opens in downtown Minneapolis.*

1973 *U.S. involvement in Vietnam War ends.*

1975

1974 *February, First meeting of the Care Guild.*

1974 *Coadjutor Archbishop Byrne dies.*

1975 *Basilica placed on National Register
of Historic Places.*

1975 *Basilica School closes.*

1975 *Archbishop Binz dies; succeeded by
Archbishop John R. Roach.*

1975 *Average U.S. income is $10,655 per year.
Pound of bread costs 42.3¢.*

1978 *Pope Paul VI dies; succeeded by Pope John Paul I,
then Pope John Paul II.*

1978 *Father Alfred Wagner becomes rector.*

1980

Architectural historian Carol Frenning started coming to the
Basilica in 1975, after moving into the parish.

"It was my neighborhood church. I remember thinking how
large it was, vast and empty. I think cavernous would be a
word I'd use. There were only about two hundred families, and
most of the people that belonged lived in nursing homes—I
think there are thirteen nursing homes in the area that the
Basilica kind of took care of. And there were maybe eighty children! It was a very shrunken existence, a parish that was in
decline. The mid-seventies were probably the low end of that
period. There was a very real danger that the building might be
torn down; the viability of it as a parish was in question.

A stuffed and tattered manila envelope marked "Here's some old
stuff" is filled with the scattered traces of one family's active relationship with the Basilica and its school. Don and Lynn Pirner, having joined the parish in 1961, had three children in the Basilica
School in the early seventies.

Included are school newspapers, hockey schedules, and religion
outlines. David Pirner played a king in a third-grade play. A summer field trip went to a farm. In 1973, altar girls! It is a paper trail
of one family's relationship with their parish church.

The Pirners, even while raising young children, found time to
become involved in the parish, experiencing some of the changes that
came from Vatican II.

"Monsignor Berntson was in Rome part of the time at
Vatican II and that influenced some of our cutting edge
attitudes about it. I remember at one time, someone said, 'Well,

Above: Sister Bernadine, on the
right, leads singers and musicians in one of the first guitar
masses at the Basilica in 1969.

Left: Immediately in front of
Monsignor Berntson are the first
altar girls to serve at the
Basilica, 1973.

Right: In 1974, a portion of the sacristy was designated as a chapel, "the intimate and energy-conscious place" for daily Mass, special weddings, and small funerals. The chapel was described in the parish newsletter as "a small contribution to the nation's effort to cut expenditures." This chapel wedding took place in 1981.

Far Right: Monsignor Terrance Berntson in 1974.

let's just blow up the place, and take out the pews! We'll have a round church with the altar in the middle.' The seventies were so turbulent that all attitudes were changing anyway. We got a general idea that we were now going to be a community, we were going to have English, and that, ideally, everybody would share equally. What could we do with this church? We had this huge main altar and all these pews. We had lots of gold and silver and everybody was talking about pottery and earthy things. The communion rail sort of got in the way of the guitars and the folk mass.

"It was very difficult for us to do anything, and the church was very poor. The best we could do was move the wooden altar out in front of the main altar. It's lucky that we were poor. Or somebody might have come up with some money to remove the pews or something worse!"

On April 23, 1973, the Sunday bulletin carried a letter from Bishop Cowley.

"It is my painful duty to wish all of you a farewell. As you know during the past year I was laid low by a crushing illness. I thought recovery to health was inevitable but I find that resignation is the only reasonable thing for me to do. . . . We are very happy to announce that my position as pastor will be assumed by Msgr. Terrance Berntson, formerly the Chancellor of the Archdiocese of Saint Paul. . . . He is a holy and a well gifted man."

Only one year later, May 5, 1974, the announcement was "Father Terrance Berntson, our pastor, is recovering well at Saint Mary's Hospital following his heart attack last week." In May, Father Berntson wrote that his period of recuperation would last a good part of the summer.

CONSTITUTION

Title

The name of this organization shall be the Basilica Care Guild of the Basilica of St. Mary.

Purpose *To serve as a coordinating body of volunteers in service to the Pastor and Parish thus to promote communication and cooperation and*

To assist the Pastor in carrying out the needs of this *of our* Parish in the fulfillment of spiritual, social, and cultural actions.

Membership ② *STRIKE*

This Guild shall be open to all Basilica (~~Women~~) Parishioners. *age (~~the eligible~~ + Confirmation) into active Body of Church unless by Board*

Officers

The officers shall be a President, Vice President, Secretary, and a Treasurer. All of the officers shall be elected at the annual meeting.

Monsignor Berntson had been pastor of St. Cecilia in St. Paul and chaplain at the College of St. Catherine, as well as chancellor of the diocese.

In 1997, the Basilica Magazine ran a story by Deanna Campbell called "A Lasting Legacy." It said, in part:

"Think back to the early 1970s. Across the nation women marched in political rallies, especially those which protested the war in Vietnam, supported the Feminist Movement, and in many ways, took the lead in social activism. Social justice issues were in the forefront of the American conscience.

" 'It was such an exciting time. Here at the Basilica, Monsignor Terrance Berntson founded an organization called the Care Guild, ' remembers Karen Harrison, an early member. 'This organization was conceived around the theme of social activism. We had a new understanding of social justice issues and were eager to make a difference within the parish and the community.'

"The Guild's first meeting in February 1974 attracted fewer than forty women. Though its mission was simply to 'assist the pastor and the staff social worker in filling the needs of the parish in the areas of spiritual, social and cultural action,' the Guild's membership and influence grew quickly. In fact, during its twenty-year history, the Guild became the most influential volunteer group in the Basilica's history.

" 'It is difficult to overstate the importance of the Care Guild's legacy to the Basilica,' says Tom Green, Basilica Director of Administration and Finance. 'Many of the programs the Guild created were the forerunners of today's very active and dynamic ministries.' "

Left: Many hands and minds go into the formation of volunteer organizations. This original draft of the Care Guild bylaws shows revision by at least three dedicated members.

Above: Some of the dedicated parishioners who made the Care Guild one of the most influential volunteer groups in the Basilica's history.

BASILICA FOOD SHELF REPORT FOR 1975

BASILICA FOOD SHELF REPORT FOR 1975

The Basilica Food Shelf opened July 1, 1975 as a walk-in center for the distributing of donated food to people in need. Two rooms on the second floor of the parish school building are used for food storage and office space.

The following is an accounting of what has transpired during that six month period.

Requests for emergency assisstance:
1,203 (1,183 at Food Shelf office
13 at Rectory
6 by telephone- home delivery)

People served:
1,639 Adults   (Some of these are counted more than once
976 Children   because of repeated requests.)

Groceries distributed:
1,202 bags of food (containing varying amounts of food
depending on client's needs.)

Approximately 800 volunteer hours were donated by members of the parish to operate the Food Shelf.

Food donated in collections prior to July 1st were used to stock the

Above: The Basilica food shelf report for its first six months of operation in 1975.

"Within three months of its founding, the Guild's membership more than tripled to 128 parishioners. They had formed five standing committees that affected virtually every aspect of the Basilica's mission in the community. The committees were: Membership and Parish Newcomers, which welcomed new parishioners, acquainted people with the Care Guild, and solicited new members; the Spiritual and Cultural Enrichment committee, which included scripture study, choral concerts and Lenten programs, and rectory open houses; Social Action committee, which established the food shelf, food collections, and sandwich ministry, and took foods to families in time of crisis; the Hospital, Nursing Homes and Home-bound committee, which visited parishioners in hospitals, at home or in nursing homes, and maintained a telephone reassurance program; the Fund Raising and Parish Needs committee, which coordinated Sunday morning coffee hour and nursery service, rummage, book, and bake sales, and other fund raising events.

" 'We started the food shelf in the basement of the rectory,' recalls Ann Reichel, a former Guild member who still participates in food shelf activities. 'Catholic Charities Branch II agreed to be our cosponsor.' "

"The sewing group made crafts to sell at Fun Fest and the Christmas Boutique; they collected Christmas gifts for parishioners in nursing homes; volunteers worked the Aquatennial

Sally Brothers, standing at left, has been making sandwiches for the food shelf and outreach ministries at the Basilica since 1973; originally the cost of the meat and bread came out of her own pocket.

Left: Peaceful picketing before the school closed in 1975. It was reported that there were fewer than one hundred students.

crowds selling popcorn, snow cones, and other goodies; they presented flowers to each mother attending Mass on Mother's Day; and they gave Thanksgiving baskets to the needy, filled partly by the proceeds of pumpkin sales in October. Newcomer receptions saw as many as fifty people attending. The Marriage Encounter program was introduced and a young adults group was organized.

"Not only did the Care Guild provide outreach to the parish, it also organized spiritual and social opportunities for all parishioners to participate in. These included activities such as Lenten programs, book discussions, retreats, musical concerts, and tours of the Minneapolis Institute of Art and the Walker Museum."

As the Care Guild expanded, the maintenance of the Basilica School became a more difficult issue. As early as 1963, Bishop Cowley had expressed concern about attracting children to the school, stating that it was less than half-filled. Other complicating factors were a general decline in interest in Catholic education, a lack of teaching nuns, and the fracturing of the Basilica neighborhood by the freeway. "The parish simply couldn't afford it," remembers Lynn Pirner. "We picketed the Archdiocesan offices. It was mothers with carloads of children, and we marched on the sidewalk in an orderly way."

On February 16, 1975, the Sunday bulletin carried a letter from Monsignor Berntson. "On February 3, 1975 the Archdiocesan Board of Education approved the recommendation of the Basilica parish council to terminate our day school effective at

Basilica Girl Scouts, 1971.

the close of the 1974–75 school year. The decision of the pastor and parish council was unanimous, the vote being 14 to 0. . . . The Board accepted our recommendations and approved the steps which we took in an effort to continue our school in existence. Those many efforts, as you know, indicated a desire for a school but an insufficiency of the necessary funding." The principal of the school, Roger Sinclair, moved to the Basilica staff as Director of the Basilica Educational Ministry.

The Basilica no longer needed its teaching sisters. Starting in the 1970s, the convent that stood in its shadow was leased out to a law firm and various treatment centers.

In June of 1978, Reverend Alfred S. Wagner became rector of the Basilica after previous pastorships in Northfield, Robbinsdale, and at St. Helena's in Minneapolis. With Father Wagner are some of the many chalices of the Basilica; most stories of their origin are forgotten.

On March 26, 1975, the Basilica of Saint Mary was designated as an historic landmark by the National Register of Historic Places. The application read, in part:

"In summary, the Basilica of Saint Mary derives its significance from three major areas. Firstly, it exemplifies great design in architecture and engineering. Designed by Masqueray, it ranks with the Cathedral of Saint Paul as an expression of Baroque influence in church architecture of the early twentieth century. Secondly, the Basilica is a testimonial to the religious movements and their roles in the development of Minnesota's heritage. And, thirdly, the building was the first such church to be proclaimed a basilica in the United States."

The application also stated that "the Basilica is an excellent state of preservation."

However, work was long overdue. In October of 1975, Father Berntson announced to the congregation that the church needed a new roof. "For decades the only work on the roof has been an occasional patching job," he said. "Gigantic amounts of water" had gotten into the area between the roof and the inside false ceiling. The plaster ceiling "is soaking into itself the humid air and causing the flaking and falling of plaster. Unless something is done immediately the inner ceiling could be destroyed in another five years." The cost of repairs was estimated at $134,000.

Water damage over the east door to the Basilica.

*I*n the mid-eighties, a brisk wind of change blew through the Basilica and its community. This is the period when stories tell of sheets of copper from the dome blowing down Highway 12, and water pouring down the inside walls during rainstorms. Prompted both by concern about the condition of the building and by a strong sense of the potential for growth embodied in the old parish and its magnificent but aging buildings, new leadership brought bold thinking and innovative and appealing ideas.

Almost immediately, the people of the Basilica community responded to these ideas with enthusiasm and with efforts to "wake the sleeping giant." By the end of the decade, the Basilica was functioning as a ceremonial space, a viable home for liturgy, and as a human-sized, albeit vast, parish church.

AT THE BASILICA	LIFE OF THE CHURCH	CIVIC LIFE
1980		
		1980 Population of Minneapolis is 370,951. Average U.S. income is $15,721 per year. Pound of bread costs 51.9¢.
1985		1982 First baseball game played in Hubert H. Humphrey Metrodome.
1985 Reverend Dennis Dease becomes rector.		1985 Average U.S. income is $18,980 per year. Pound of bread costs 71¢.
1990		

In the summer of 1985, Father Dennis Dease left the staff of the Saint Paul Seminary to begin service as the rector of the Basilica of Saint Mary. It was the beginning of a time of great change.

"It was a thrill for me to go to the Basilica. Up to that point in my life, it was the happiest assignment I'd ever had. When I started, the parish was in pretty tough shape financially, and the numbers had been dwindling. It was down to nine hundred registered households. That first fall, I invited Jay Hunstiger to come as liturgist, and he was a marvelous influence on the parish. He raised the quality of music and liturgy by many multiples over the course of his first year or two there. He also used liturgy as a way of forming community. When I left in 1991, we had grown from nine hundred to nineteen hundred and fifty.

"There are two major themes in the late eighties at the Basilica. The first is a theme of astonishing growth and engagement in the parish itself. There was some considerable distance to go; it's been said that in 1985 you could shoot a cannon through the church on Sunday and not hit anybody.

"But it was absolutely unique as a parish. It had this absolutely grand old architecture that made it a landmark in not only downtown Minneapolis, but throughout the region. And it's located on Hennepin Avenue, right on the edge of downtown, as well as on a major interstate freeway, where tens of thousands of people pass every day. But part of what makes the Basilica unique is the constituency. The people of the Basilica are what made it the happiest years in my life as a priest. And they were such a varied group that one might think this group would never gel. Looking out at the people at Mass on Sunday, I would see somebody who was obviously a homeless woman sitting next to a woman in a mink coat.

"I think a lot of people were attracted to the Basilica because of the combination of ministries. A lot of people were attracted purely by the architecture and the beautiful building; they liked to worship in a beautiful building and the Basilica is magnificent. A lot were attracted by the ministry to the poor, especially Catholics that tend to be more socially activistic. A lot were attracted by the involvement with the arts, especially Catholics for whom beauty is an essential way of finding God in their lives. A lot were attracted by the liturgy and we also worked very hard on the homilies, too. We tried to deliver homilies that were thoughtful and pressed the envelope a bit. Our

In most old and beautiful places, there is a ghost story. Dr. Kim Kasling came to the Basilica as the organist and music director in 1981. As all church musicians know, filling a church with music requires rehearsing in the space when it is quiet and empty.

"My second week here, I went downstairs on a Saturday night to prepare something. And I turned around and looked out at the huge space, with almost no lights on, and I just about dropped my teeth. I could swear that there was a figure sitting right at the crossing all in white. Well, I just ran, I just ran upstairs. Father Wagner was the pastor then, and he said he'd come down and look. He did. Nothing was there, of course. And he said that had happened before. They thought it was Bishop Cowley down there."

Above: The 1983 ordination day of Deacon George Babcock, whose class marked the tenth anniversary of the diaconate program in the archdiocese. The work of deacons is critical to the programs of the Basilica.

hope was to send people on their way thinking.

"Some people were attracted to all of those things, but I think most people focused in on one or the other. And in the process they kind of liked the other things that were going on, too. The liturgy became the integrating experience and everybody shared that in common."

The staff was small; lay leadership was critical as the number of members grew.

"Much of the work was being done by the Care Guild who organized the laity for social services, nursing home coverage, working with the poor people who would come in for various forms of assistance. Deacon George Babcock was the staff coordinator of all those programs; he did a marvelous job. And he involved hundreds of parishioners in those social service ministries through the Care Guild. Jay Hunstiger coordinated worship as the minister of worship, and he involved literally hundreds of parishioners.

"In some ways, having the work done by the parishioners

themselves is what delivers the sense of ownership to people and it builds the community and forges familial kinds of bonds. Each person could find a chance to make some human connections and to be part of a community that I think worked hard at caring."

One of the early community-building efforts involved hospitality, Jay Hunstiger recalls.

"When I started, they did hospitality after the nine-thirty Mass, one Mass per Sunday, every week. And it was done in the rectory in the copy machine room, which was maybe five feet by eight feet. So we decided we would start in the sacristy after the nine-thirty. Within a month we had maximized the space, so we moved it to the back of the church. We took out some pews and immediately people at the eleven o'clock Mass began saying, 'Well, why can't we have it?' And then the eight o'clock people said that. And the four-thirty. So we expanded it, largely under the direction of Shelby Logeais. She was able to get it set up where we were doing sixty-five dozen donuts a weekend, and twelve gallons of cider and 450 cups of coffee, after every Mass in the back of the church, without a sink, without a kitchen!

And people so desperately wanted a community that, as this thing built, they just filled the whole back part of the church, and up the side aisles.

"The first Holy Week, for Palm Sunday, I invited people to be part of a procession inside the church. It was kind of slow going. But the second year, attendance started to pick up because people

Father Dease shares one of his fondest memories of the Basilica.

Above: Decorating for Advent.

Left: Advent wreath in the Basilica.

"We would invite the parish family to come in and decorate the Basilica for Christmas. We would order a million pizzas and cases of Coke and people would come in, old and young. Young parents would bring their kids, and you'd have people who were in their nineties, and every color of the rainbow and from every walk of life. We would play some Christmas music over the PA system and they would go to work, and just transform the place. It looked like something out of a Charles Dickens story."

New art acquisitions were made for the Basilica, including a new wrought iron icon stand, made by Mark Nichols, new vestments by Phyllis Lehmberg Ecclesiastical Needlework, and a sanctuary lamp from the Saint Paul Seminary Chapel.

While the Basilica was filling up with new parishioners, a vibrant liturgy, and revitalized programming, the time had come for

remembered the previous Holy Week. By the third year, during the Palm Sunday procession at the nine-thirty Mass, the tail met the head and we actually came to a crashing halt. It was so wonderful. The same thing happened at the eleven thirty. Then finally, after that year, we did the processions so they would go down the side aisle, all the way through the ambulatory, through the choir stalls and back around, just to get all the people in. It was the biggest loop we could get in the church."

Maybe prayer, or just the habit of being there.' That must have been around 1989 or 1990.

"One morning I came in for Mass and the organist, Dr. Kim Kasling, was there, and he said, 'I want you to come out and take a look in the sanctuary.' Just between the organ and the altar, a huge hunk of plaster had fallen from way up inside the dome. If it had hit someone, that kind of weight would have killed them. The plaster was becoming wet and losing its cohesiveness."

As Carol Frenning tells the story, "The Basilica hired the architectural firm of Swanke, Hayden, Connell—the same people who restored the Statue of Liberty—to survey the damage. Walls and wooden support beams were soggy and rotten with water damage. Only four of over one hundred supports that connect the Basilica's three cement floors were intact. While the work was being done, construction workers discovered that the rose windows were actually holding the supporting walls, not the other way around."

major work on its aged building. Smaller repairs would no longer suffice. Time, and design flaws, threatened the future of the landmark structure.

Father Dease recalls.

"The capital campaign was to seal the envelope and stabilize the structure. I used to hear those words of our engineer in my sleep at night. You have to 'seal the envelope and stabilize the structure.' Water was seeping in through our very complex roof system and freezing and moving stones out to the point where they could have pushed out of the tower of the dome and catapulted off the roof. Also the suspended plaster ceiling—I asked the engineer one day, 'What is holding that ceiling and that arch up there?' The engineer told me, 'It beats me, Father.

A fifty-year-old layer of linseed oil is removed from the rose window at the south end of the Basilica in July 1989. At the same time, the thick glass installed originally as an outside layer was removed. Clear contemporary glass brightened the rose window colors from inside the Basilica. "We found the colors darting all around the back of the church," remembers Jay Hunstiger.

Left: Accumulated water damage endangered the painting of Saint Mark, one of four oil-on-canvas portraits of the Evangelists in the dome over the high altar.

Parishioner Manny Villafana helped organize the funding for repairs and the hiring of architects. The church leadership had tremendous cooperation from the construction workers who worked on the church in the late eighties and early nineties. McGough Construction, for example, repainted their normally-red scaffolding so that it would blend in more with the church's interior architecture.

Jay Hunstiger recalls the summer flood of 1987.

"When we put in the new hymnals, we had to have all new racks made for them. The night that we put those racks in with parishioners came the big summer flood of 1987. Water was pouring into the Basilica; people couldn't even get out of the church. There was thunder and lightning and the rose windows were pouring in water. Water down the walls. We had buckets and huge, huge amounts of water coming in.

"This was the typical problem that we had, and we were saying, 'We've got to do something fast because this building will not be standing in ten years if we allow this kind of deterioration to continue.' We actually said that to people: 'If you want this building here, if you don't want just a marker on Hennepin Avenue that says this is where the Basilica stood, you've got to come forward. You've got to do your part.' "

Of the Basilica outreach programs, Jay Hunstiger said, "We're open every day of the year for anyone who wants to come in, if only to get warm. If some of them sleep, we tell ourselves they just nodded off after their prayer."

-100-

"About the mid-eighties, a major focus of Catholic identity in the west metro area started to settle on the Basilica. And this church began to acquire a whole lot more identity as a cathedral church."
—Father Michael O'Connell

Needlepoint bench covers, shown here with longtime parishioner Margaret Morris, were stitched by church volunteers in the 1990s.

Franchelle Mullin, interior designer and parishioner, remembers the painstaking creation of needlepoint kneelers for the Mary chapel.

"In 1989, the environment committee thought it time to begin using the Mary Chapel as a chapel (the space was being used for storage) and moved the Mary statue from the side vestibule of the sanctuary to the chapel. To help create a space of reflection, kneelers and benches were suggested.

"After visiting our neighbor church St. Mark's Cathedral and talking to their needlepoint volunteers under the guidance of David Peterson, our committee decided to hire Katherine Parfet of Inver Grove Heights to design canvases for our Cathedral using the symbols of Mary depicted in the interior of the church. Many committee hours were spent working with Katherine to create just the right design and colors. The result was so intricate and complicated that it took almost a year, counting and painting each stitch, for her to complete the five canvases.

Ruth Mullin, Sue Hayes, Susie Kennedy, Janet Sawyer and Rose Litzinger spent several months to a year or more to complete each piece. What a pleasure it was for them to see their work completed and installed in the Mary Chapel."

The Saint Vincent de Paul Society, founded in France in 1833, is an international Catholic organization that reaches out to the poor on an individual basis. The Basilica chapter provides direct support with food, shelter problems, and clothing. Volunteer mentors work with participants to help stabilize their lives and find good jobs.

Father Dease remembers a time in the eighties when Bishop Lawrence Welsh of Spokane, Washington was in residence at the Basilica and doing volunteer work at the Branch II soup kitchen.

"Nobody was better with the poor than he was. Well, at one point we asked him to celebrate the main Easter Sunday Mass, which was the grandest celebration of the year for us. He presided over that in his crosier and miter and the Basilica was just packed with people. At the end, he was processing out with all his regalia, and one of the clients from the soup kitchen was in the church. And as the Bishop was coming down the aisle in all his regalia, this guy shouted out, 'Larry! I didn't know you worked here!'

"Well, it was the kind of thing that would be a shock to some churches, but at the Basilica, well, it was just the way church should be. Larry told that story for years afterward on himself."

Plasterers and painters replaced and repaired water damaged plaster in the dome.

Above: In 1991, the Minnesota Twins won the World Series and the Basilica celebrated along with the rest of the city. The parade went right down Hennepin Avenue.

*A*t the Basilica of Saint Mary, the nineties were years of acceleration, growth, excitement … and a lot of repair. Energetically seeking the involvement of long-time parishioners and new faces, particularly young faces, the Basilica seemed to sprout new programs, new ideas, new artworks, new energies, as if the ever-present construction workers were not only replacing and refreshing the weakened sections of Masqueray's old dome, and preparing the undercroft for the future, but also carrying in loads of energy and enthusiasm.

The Basilica was becoming a public space again, as well as a home for private worship and a house for attentive liturgy. Rooting for the Twins and attending small-scale evening prayer services. Repainting the glorious interior dome and posing for pictures as its massive cap was lifted off the top. Encouraging ushers to smile at children on Sunday mornings and helping to start a Jeremiah Program to help change the lives of the poor.

Retaining and strengthening its core as a home for worship, the Basilica strengthened its position as a public entity. Its people served the poor, formed ecumenical ties with other denominations, sought out and welcomed the arts, and attracted droves of young energetic newcomers. Some may have first been attracted by the building's pomp, but many stayed because of the building's people.

A worker's picnic on-site in the nineties.

AT THE BASILICA	LIFE OF THE CHURCH	CIVIC LIFE

1990

1991 Father Michael O'Connell becomes rector.

1991 Friends of the Basilica founded.

1991–1993 Renovation of dome.

1990 Population of Minneapolis is 368,383. Average U.S. income is $23,258 per year. Pound of bread costs 72¢.

1992 Archbishop Roach retires; succeeded by Archbishop Harry J. Flynn.

1991 Persian Gulf War.

1995

1995 Average U.S. income is $27,440 per year. Pound of bread costs 78.2 cents.

1998 New bells hung in Basilica bell tower.

1999 July, Construction begins on undercroft.

1999 Partnership initiated with Ascension Parish, north Minneapolis.

2000

Growth is easily represented in numbers, and in the late eighties and nineties, the number of parishioners was certainly rising. Real growth involves not just numbers but more people who decide to become involved. Trustee Joanne Provo was one of those people. She is shown here with the altar dedicated to St. Therese of Lisieux. The Italian mosaic ceiling illustrates the concept of self-sacrifice as a mother pelican feeding her young with her blood.

"I joined the Basilica in 1989. I'm from this area but moved back from Chicago. At the time I really was looking for a place that was very large, where I could get lost in the crowd. I had a very demanding job, and I have a tendency to get too involved—I just didn't want to get pegged for anything. But I quickly found out that this was not the kind of parish you could hide out in.

"At that time I went to the nine-thirty Mass, and there was nobody there. I had a pew to myself; it was very low key. Everybody knew everybody's face, but I didn't ever stick around to have coffee or conversation. Occasionally I would attend early Mass, and they were in sorry need of eucharistic ministers and people to help, because there wasn't a very big crowd there, either. So I was approached to be a eucharistic minister and I think shortly thereafter I became part of the finance committee. Shortly after that I co-chaired the strategic planning committee. In the midst of that, Father O'Connell asked me to become a trustee, so I became, I believe, the youngest trustee this place has ever had. The next thing I was chairing the undercroft committee and serving on special events committees and I don't even know what all else. My plan to stay in the pew and be anonymous really changed."

Father Michael O'Connell is shown with the baptismal font, placed near the main entrance to symbolize entry into the faith through the sacrament of baptism.

In early 1991, Father Michael O'Connell came to the Basilica of Saint Mary as rector when Father Dease was appointed as president of the University of Saint Thomas. Father O'Connell had previously been Vicar General and Moderator of the Curia for the Archdiocese of Saint Paul and Minneapolis and, for sixteen years, the pastor of the Church of St. Cecilia in St. Paul.

"Well, first of all I was attracted to the classical beauty of the building. I love the cultural emphasis they had here, the concerts and the quality of the music. The social justice was a wonderful thing, so strong. And the liturgy was beautiful and I cared about that. I had an intuition that I could build on all that. And I was drawn to the challenge of the fund raising. The construction itself began about four months after I got here, and the number to raise became nine and a half million dollars.

"The number had gone up and, at about the same time we started to understand the size of our task, we hired Terri Ashmore as our development director. We had to build a fairly sophisticated development office from scratch, and that's something I don't think any other congregation has had to do. We had to create major events around the year, the purpose of which was to reach out beyond the parish boundaries and create occasions when non-parishioners could be attracted to us and hear our story and develop interest in us. The Block Party is a very good example of that. The annual Christmas concert with the Minnesota Orchestra and Chorale doing the Messiah is another good example. We have an annual St. Paul Saints baseball game benefit; we've done a number of large events.

"The purpose of it is to create a visibility in the community and get a lot of people's interest, develop loyalty, and raise money. Our development office has worked hard to come to terms with an unusual reality. And that is that if we were going to raise the kind of money that was necessary, we were going to have to raise more than half of it from people who were not parishioners. But we accepted the challenge. So the end of this story is that our development office did in fact set up a whole mechanism and network of relationships. When we finished the first campaign, we raised nine and a half million dollars; about five million of that came from non-parishioners. The money that did come from our parishioners was a big stretch, too, because we're talking about a lot of young adults who had never made pledges before, to anything.

"Then, within the same eight year period, we had a second capital campaign for the undercroft. We wanted to finally do what those other people started to do effectively ten years before. That's a good story. Back in 1984 or 1985, there was a committee that got together and spent hundreds of hours planning to get additional programmatic space, in the basement of the church. They needed space for bathrooms, for education, for a gathering space, a space to serve food. They had an architect and a model. Then somewhere in 1987 or so, the structural problems upstairs started to manifest themselves, and essentially that undercroft plan had to be put aside.

"It wasn't until 1997 or 1998 that we once again revisited the need for increased program space. It was for all the same reasons, plus we need a space that is large inside and hospitable for serving the poor. We've never had that kind of space here. In November of 1998, we launched a campaign to raise a little over six million dollars, and that was done by January of 2000.

"All of our programs, the giving and the volunteer programs (we have over two thousand volunteers a year in our various efforts) and the outreach programs, they all fall under the Biblical idea of stewardship. Catholics used to think of stewardship as a Protestant word. Yet in the last twenty years, the Roman Catholic church has appropriated that term from the Bible, and understands it as the spiritual base for why we give back to God from the gifts God has given us.

"There's a fundamental acknowledgment that God gave us everything we have in the first place. Our obligation is to give back generously and gratefully, in terms of helping the ongoing co-creation. This theology and spirituality stands very powerfully at the heart and soul of what we preach, teach, and believe here.

"Stewardship shows itself in the annual growth of our volunteers, who are people in our congregation who are involved in the life of the parish, apart from their attendance at liturgy. That shows a sense of ownership and commitment and investment that speaks deeply to that spiritual reality of giving, since often our time is more precious than money. And I think the other manifestation of it has been a phenomenal growth in terms of annual giving and capital giving. A lot of that is based in gratitude, in people's recognition that they've been gifted, especially in belonging to the Basilica community."

In the late eighties, the condition of the building clearly needed to be addressed. Architectural historian Carol Frenning wanted to help. She founded an organization separate from the church, the Friends of the Basilica.

"What needed to be done was recapture the kind of atmosphere that would help people become aware of the plight of this historical site. Also we could solicit the financial help of people in the community, outside the parish, who loved the building. That's why the Friends of the Basilica began.

"My friend, Fran Mullin, an interior designer and I started the project together and it took us two years to work out all the details, many while walking around Lake of the Isles. We started with a homecoming celebrating a lot of memories for people who attended school or were married at the Basilica. A board was formed, goals were set and a not-for-profit status was established. Our main trust was educational, simply because we needed to get the story out. We wanted people to understand the historical significance of the building. There had been some very serious talk about abandoning the building, or tearing it down.

"I'm very proud that the Friends of the Basilica exists. There have been so many people that have been touched by it and by the work that they've done. For example, the docent program under the auspices of the Friends has been a great service to the Basilica community and a link to the community at large."

In the early nineties, one parishioner at the Basilica was Brenda Wehle, a leading actress in the Guthrie Theater's acting company. Father O'Connell asked her to consider becoming a lector at the Basilica, and then to help other lectors read more effectively.

"His argument was that I had been given a gift and the parish could use the gift in spreading the word of God, for people to be able to hear the word of God. Father Michael felt that the word was the most important communication during the Mass.

"The experience of reading at the Basilica is an act of balancing sheer terror with responsibility. When you process in, it feels like a parade. You seem to be in the middle of everyone and then you get further and further away. You know that you're speaking the word of God and it's coming through you. There's a dove, the Holy Spirit, just above the pulpit and my image became that this dove would send the words down through me. That's one way I could remove myself from the terror of being a listener to the word of God and the speaker at the same time.

"Later Michael had the idea of creating what he called the lector choir; he felt so strongly about reading that he felt it should be treated no less importantly than the Basilica choir. We devised, with Johan (van Parys, Director of Worship) a training cycle. We celebrated the readings and it was wonderful. I would meet with the lectors every Wednesday on my Guthrie dinner break, between rehearsals."

In the mid-nineties, the Basilica acquired a new nativity set. Joanne Provo remembers.

Jay Hunstiger looked for new art for the rapidly growing Basilica.

"The Sisters of the Order of St. Benedict had a set of wooden angels, and I told them we'd love to have them in the Basilica because things are happening there, it's open all the time, people can see and appreciate them. We went up to St. Ben's, parishioners on a bus, and we loaded the angels up and afterwards McGough Construction installed them all for free on a down day. Then we had a big dedication service and evensong service. We invited the nuns and they brought 140 sisters down from St. Ben's, and they were just ecstatic to see them being used."

"We got some folks together to put together a creche. There was a statue that they were going to buy out of a catalog, and there was a woman in the creche scene. It was a woman, and it was the first time I'd ever seen a woman in the nativity scene, other than Mary. I found a couple whom I knew from the church, Irene and Dominic Mandile, and I asked them if they would go in with me, and they did, and we were able to dedicate it. So I dedicated it to my dad, who is dead, and my mom. The first year, my mom came to midnight Mass and she was so emotional and so moved. We went back after Mass and there was this creche scene and the straw and there was this lady with the little water pitcher. Now, for the next however many Christmases I'm here, I'll see it. It's a huge church, but there's a little piece of it dedicated to my mom and dad."

Religious education acquired a new name in the nineties—faith formation— and at the Basilica, it became one of the most important initiatives for the future. Father O'Connell tells the story. "It's too simplistic," he smiles, "but here's how I tell it."

"We deliberately and intentionally started out back in 1995 to grow this parish in terms of more young adults with the Block Party. And it worked. And those young adults came here and then they started to get married. We went up to one hundred and twenty marriages a year; we got overwhelmed on the marriages. And then they started having kids. And then they started to stick around with their kids. Then the baptisms went out of sight.

"Then in 1998, we did a demographic study of the parish, and we were all astounded to find that there were six hundred kids under the age of three. We'd been aware of an ever-increasing number of older children because every year our religious education programming was exploding. Every year you added at least a third more, especially kindergarten through sixth grade. Now, they take over every room in the school and the basement of Cowley.

"I would say that for a religious education program that is not located in a parochial school, it's as good as I've ever seen.

It's extremely well thought-out. There are talented, committed parents on oversight committees and advisory committees and they are fierce in terms of making sure that our programming is quality. They want our kids to be highly visible in the midst of our community. George Barrett is our Director of Education and Faith Formation, a terrific leader in these areas.

"Then back in '92 or '93, I wanted to have state of the art childcare here on Sunday mornings. So we put together an excellent childcare program that started to attract families with little kids. If you wanted to, you could go to the nine-thirty Mass, leave your child in childcare, then go down to the Loring for brunch. It might be the only hour in the week that you spent with each other! And out of that grew a Montessori religious education program, the Good Shepherd. It takes hundreds of hours in training of your teachers; the commitment is unbelievable. But the parents love it. I'm proud of our faith formation program."

WHEN IT RAINS, IT POURS.

Help restore the Basilica of St. Mary.

Far left: Note the banner "Help Us Restore The Dome." Many did.

Left: Advertising during the restoration period.

Below: A rooftop picnic for workers and staff.

Work began on the restoration of the Basilica's dome in 1991. Scaffolding was put up in the basement and around the altar, ultimately reaching to the inside of the dome. The dome was taken apart piece by piece, workers building the replacements under it as they took each piece off and then installing a new copper roof over the whole thing, so that the Basilica actually has two roofs. The water-damaged plaster and wood was replaced and the entire outside of the building sealed to prevent water damage in the future. The ten thousand pound copper lantern portion was lifted down by crane by McGough Construction.

The Blessing of the Animals, held on or near the feastday of St. Francis of Assisi, began as a Basilica celebration and, in the mid-nineties, became an ecumenical program with St. Mark's Cathedral and Hennepin Avenue Methodist Church. Over the years, everything from dogs and cats to penguins to pigs have been brought by their owners to church. A snow leopard and a tiger have been blessed. The portion of the ceremony in Loring Park has featured an elephant, exotic cats, and a camel. Parishioner Diana Gulden first attended the Blessing of the Animals, and then volunteered. She was elected parish council chair in 1999.

"It's absolutely magical. They're happy to be there, and they want to talk about their animals. Each church has its own service and then we all process into Loring Park and have a festival. The first year we did this, it was a lovely Sunday afternoon. The mounted police were our escort and as we processed from the Basilica, we turned the corner in front of the Loring Bar and Café. There were all these sophisticated people sitting out at the tables. Around the corner came the horses, and then came our liturgical director Johan in flowing robes carrying this enormous cross overhead followed by hundreds and hundreds of people with dogs and cats. Those people couldn't believe what they were seeing! Even if you're not part of it, you're touched by it."

In 1999, the Basilica of Saint Mary and the northside Church of the Ascension formed a partnership, sharing, among other things, the pastor. "Call me a Pollyanna," says Father O'Connell, "but I think we can turn things around—get the Ascension parish back to being a shining light in the city, as it once was. There used to be three thousand families here, all kinds of programs, a wonderful community. And we can work with the neighborhood to be a force for good, help to rebuild this north side, make it a better place for everyone. We can make this Ascension block a focal point for the community, be real leaders."

Within the Basilica, parish growth throughout the nineties continued at a fast pace. Trustee Joanne Provo looks back.

"When Michael O'Connell came, he had this vision of four thousand by two thousand. He was thinking we should have four thousand parishioners, or households, by the year 2000. I remember this was in the early nineties, and sitting around the finance committee, we were saying wow! How can we handle that kind of growth? We probably had fifteen hundred households at that point. But he really had a vision to grow."

"We're a unique parish in that we draw from a large geographic distribution. The majority of our folks come from outside this particular geographic parish. People drive from Burnsville, Eden Prairie, Plymouth, Stillwater to come to Mass here. While we are a great community, we're really not a community parish geographically. We are not isolated by geographic distinctions."

After twenty-some years of leasing the old convent building to others, the Basilica reclaimed it in 1993 to house its growing religious education programs and development office. It was named the Bishop Leonard Cowley Center.

Left: The Basilica's Father Joe Whalen delivers the homily in front of the elaborately carved altar at Church of the Ascension.

Above: Father O'Connell on the steps at Ascension.

Carolyn Baldus is shown here with the Calvary grouping near the high altar at the Basilica. The life-size crucifix was carved in place by John Garratti of St. Paul in 1924. The sculpture lacks the customary Mary Magdalene figure; it is said that the observer is meant to take her place. The tableau was modeled after a miraculous crucifix in Lympia, Spain.

February 4, 1994 was a big night in the life of parishioner Carolyn Baldus. Newly arrived in the Twin Cities from Washington, D.C., a friend suggested to Carolyn that she attend something called Avenues, a young people's group, at the Basilica.

"So I asked my friend, 'Do you think that's worth going to or is it just kind of a churchy singles thing that I wouldn't really like?' He said I should go, that I'd probably meet some interesting people there. I'm really glad I took his advice, because that night I met my husband!

"And on that same day, I was asked if I would consider helping with a project they were putting together. They told me it was a little church party. Well, that became the Basilica Block Party. That led to many, many new friends. I had been in the Twin Cities for just about a year at that point and didn't know many people. That really changed the direction of my life.

"I loved being part of the initial committee, but there was some doubt that we could really do this. But so many people came together with such strong energies and such a desire to create something that was really positive, that was really good, that was really fun.

The Basilica Block Party is billed as "a party of a higher order."

"The first year, well, in a way, you never know what to expect until you're actually in the middle of it. I remember it was four o'clock and we were going to open the gates at five, and all of a sudden we realized, people were milling all around. We had a ticketed event but forgot that we actually had to close the gates in order to open them. And I remember standing on the parking ramp and watching the floods of people coming in. My heart was just racing thinking, 'Oh, we've done it, after all this hard work.'

And a lot of the bands have become really fond of Father O'Connell. One year, the lead singer of Big Head Todd called and asked if he would come to the Target Center and introduce him for their concert there.

The First Annual Block Party, held in 1995, netted $100,000 toward the reduction of the Basilica 2000 debt. In following years, thousands volunteered to work at the event, and tens of thousands attended the several nights of concerts on the Basilica grounds.

Father Dease remembers Don Piazza, a central figure at the Basilica. At the time of Piazza's death in 1996, Father O'Connell said that Piazza had "seen many come and many go and he knew that it wasn't how much you accomplished but the quality of life you shared and gave that really mattered."

"Don worked there from the time he was a child until the time he died; that was his only employment, the Basilica, as sacristan, security, custodial, as this or that. He was the general factotum, but he was one of those people that captured the heart and the soul and the spirit of the Basilica. There was no guile in him. He was pure kindness, and was supremely buoyant.

"He had a withered arm from polio as a youngster, and he was always unkempt. Let's say he was sartorially challenged. When Jay (Hunstiger) came, he put a purple alb on Don so that when Don was working as sacristan and moving through the nave and sanctuary during church services, he always had that purple alb on. And occasionally Jay changed his colors with the liturgy. Well, one time a cardinal from the Philippines came to the Basilica to say Mass for the local Filipino community. He came into the sacristy with his scarlet robes on, and in came Don Piazza. He had a scarlet alb on and I remember that the cardinal looked, and then looked again, trying to figure out what level of dignitary this person was.

"And, at the Basilica, he *was* a dignitary.

In April 1997, ground was broken for the Jeremiah Program, a single-mother family residence and support program across the street from the Basilica. It was the result of an ecumenical and public/private collaboration that began, for Father Michael O'Connell, in a conversation with the Minneapolis mayor.

"I was attending Father Dennis Dease's inauguration at the University of Saint Thomas in September of 1991 and struck up a conversation with the woman standing next to me. It turned out she was Sharon Sayles Belton, who was then president of the city council. Upon learning that I was recently installed as rector of the Basilica, she immediately commissioned me with a challenge.

" 'Unless you and the other pastors of the city make a determined effort to make your congregations strong, and unless you exercise a strong moral voice in the city, our city will fail.' "

Later that month, O'Connell was visiting with a theologian friend who, in the course of a discussion about inner city challenges, cited a verse from Jeremiah 29:7:

"Seek the well-being of the city to which I have sent you; pray for it to the Lord. For in its well-being you shall find your own."

There was an immediate convergence of that quotation and what the soon-to-be mayor had said. Sayles Belton stimulated a much broader vision of what the Basilica should be as an inner-city church.

"I started to see the bigger vision for the parish, and we started calling it the Jeremiah vision, as distinct from the Jeremiah Program."

The Jeremiah Program is a joint venture whose purpose is to provide a safe, quality living environment for single mothers and their families while they attend school and gain the skills to move on to employment and independent living. It is a partnership between seven downtown churches, the business community, five schools in the neighborhood, government, and the neighborhood association.

"The primary initiative for the Jeremiah Program came from

the Basilica. And I think a program like that demonstrates that when we said that we had a vision—to seek the well-being in the city—the community believed us. They can see how we have reached out into the community, well beyond the boundaries of our own parishioners, to make positive contributions to the city.

"Because it's a cathedral, because it's visible and accessible, the parish has to think out past its boundaries and assure a position of significance and leadership in the community. It has to establish a strong significant moral presence in the city, and for me, it's about caring for kids.

"That's what it keeps coming down to. It's always about children. And if it's about children, it's about the future, and it's about doing things to make the future a hopeful place for kids.

"Our outreach has changed since welfare reform really kicked in around 1997. We are refocusing our outreach much more to

empowerment programs. Programs that give a hand up, rather than a hand out, are much more effective. So, under the leadership of Janice Anderson, director of Social Outreach, we've clearly begun to refocus our outreach ministry in programs like employment counseling, life skills counseling, housing issues, mentoring. The Hopemaker program is a perfect example of a program led by volunteers. And our administrator Tom Green really invented the employment ministry at the Basilica. We pool the names of the unemployed in the parish and get people who are looking to employ people and try to connect them.

Tom Green, Director of Administration and Finance, joined the Basilica staff in 1989. Attending to all the church's management needs during its time of unparallelled growth, budgets, staffing, and fund raising, he also started the Basilica's stewardship programs and other critical ongoing efforts.

Above left: Mayor Sayles Belton and Father O'Connell at the ground breaking for the eighteen-unit Jeremiah Program apartment building.

Above: One of the first proud graduates of the Jeremiah Program.

"To fill this space with music is an incredible feeling. The glory of the Basilica is that the building plays back to you. There is no echo in the Basilica but there is a wonderful acoustical decay envelope. Because of the shape of the building, the sound begins at its source, and goes out like a huge long cone until it dissipates. It doesn't echo back and forth, so it's the rarest of the rare. You can get clarity and yet with large things, you get this tremendous tidal wave of sound. For an organist, it's as good as it gets."
—Dr. Kim Kasling

Basilica organist Dr. Kim Kasling started with a choir of twenty-five and two youth choirs, and in nearly twenty years has seen enormous program growth.

"Since the late seventies and early eighties, it's been altogether a growth situation. Much more than any other Catholic church in the state, we've become one of the major venues for both in-house and visiting choral and instrumental programs, so that we now have the best and strongest such profile of any church in town.

"It's largely due to our love and promotion of that kind of thing at the Basilica and the incredible acoustical environment we offer here. At one point, we had a brass festival, with the brass departments from all the colleges in the upper Midwest, including Wisconsin and the Dakotas. We had about 130 brass players. I swear you could hear it south of Richfield. It was thrilling.

"One high point was the arrival of the world famous King's College Choir of men and boys. We did a little homework in advance of their coming and found out what their colors are, and we had banners up for that. I remember the conductor turning to the packed crowd and saying, 'We feel more at home here than any other place we've come in North America.'

"We've also been able to bring in-house groups in residence, and this is a rare and wonderful thing. The Rose Ensemble, our current artists-in-residence, gives us all kinds of song, beautiful medieval and Renaissance music, as part of our Liturgical series. And the Minnesota Sinfonia found a home here, providing free concerts.

"Teri Larson started several new choirs. We have our resident groups, a full mixed choir and a children's choir. We have a chamber choir, and what's called a schola—a small group of trained, schooled singers. It's kind of like looking in a mirror and seeing multiple reflections. You have the large group and then they become more intimate in size and scope.

"We've never had a paid choir, although most big churches have a paid core of professionals. Everybody is in this choir, all ages, all walks of life. And they all share a bedrock vision of Christian faith and a love of choral music. They have their own sense of very tight community, within the larger community. For example, we had a wonderful time on our European tour in 1999; there were two busloads of us clanking all over the place. A lot of people have found a double home that way."

Teri Larson has expanded the music ministry by forming an International Choir, a children's choir, and greatly increasing the number of singers at the Basilica. "Weaving life with music is what I enjoy. I want to feed people with music—to draw them closer to God. It's what I was born to do."

Left and opposite: The Basilica choirs are led by Director of Music, Teri Larson.

Above: The "11:30 Sunday" group. Original member Chris Jordan began singing at the Basilica in 1976.

Above: Installation of the bells.

Right: Details of the casting.

In the mid-nineties, the Basilica of Saint Mary, through the generosity of an anonymous donor, began to seek a set of bells for its empty west tower. The historic bell from the Immaculate Conception church hung in the east tower. Director of Worship Johan van Parys served as the staff liaison for the bell project.

"Although our city is very noisy, there was still an acoustical void in Minneapolis. We lacked the beautiful sound of bells. Coming from Europe where the landscape is acoustically marked by bells, I found this very, very surprising. Thankfully, a generous donor took great interest in bells and after magnificent research provided us with a set of six bells.

"The process of choosing bells involves decisions in terms of foundry, carillon versus swinging bells, number and tone of the bells. These decisions need to be made with the size of the bell tower and the ethos of the building in mind. Since the bells are lifted into the tower through the windows, they too help define the size and thus the tone of the bells.

"Traditionally the church has named bells after saints. When the bells ring, they become the voice of the saints calling the people to worship. We decided that we would select names of the saints of the Americas, because in our church itself, everything is European—all the statues, all the windows. Historically it's very understandable, but I think it's time to walk a diverse path and to claim the fact that the Americas have produced saints too. We have three male saints, three female saints, we have religious and lay people, we have Native American, African American, Latin, Canadian representation."

The Basilica bells, poured in 1998 and rung for the first time at Christmas liturgies in 1998, are Saint Elizabeth Ann Seton, Blessed Juan Diego, Blessed Katharine Drexel, Blessed Kateri Tekawitha, Blessed Andre Bessette, and Blessed Pierre Toussaint.

"When they were installed and they rang for the very first time, I was incredibly moved. I don't think I'll ever forget that moment. When I hear all six ringing, I hear the communion of saints."

Father O'Connell and Rabbi Joseph Edelheit of Temple Israel won the 1999 Preus Award for their outstanding contributions to Jewish-Christian relations, furthering a long cooperation between the two houses of worship. Their relationship is both professional and personal, says Father O'Connell.

Temple Israel and Basilica of Saint Mary members outside Jerusalem in 1996.

"We're both dedicated to the principle of ecumenism, and we've done a lot of things together and in the midst of it, we have become very close friends. It really started with a benefit concert in 1993. We had ten or fifteen people from both congregations as an organizing committee, and Dave Brubeck packed Orchestra Hall. All of a sudden we had a wonderful relationship. Rabbi Edelheit and I started an interfaith study series between our two congregations and in those classes, our friendship allows us to speak very candidly and very plainly. That's very empowering and, I think, sometimes startling, to see a priest and rabbi talking plainly about issues on which they disagree. But what they see is a friendship that encourages honest dialogue. A willingness to speak and a willingness to listen and a mutual willingness to grow.

"Our colleagues at other churches wanted to get in on it so now it's a ten congregation group that meets every fall; that's the Downtown Interfaith Study Series.

"Then Rabbi and I, four years in a row, took a planeload of people to the Holocaust Museum in Washington, D.C. We took congregants, rabbis, priests, ministers, and in the final year we took teachers. As a result of that, we were invited by the museum to consider being the first Christian-Jewish congregation to establish a memorial at the museum. At the Basilica, we chose to raise the funds for that in Good Friday evening collections, which is quite startling. And the first one was also the second night of Passover; Rabbi Edelheit was with us for that collection. That is unheard of.

"We also did a joint pilgrimage to Israel and in 2000 we're taking forty-five people to Eastern Europe and to Rome."

Johan M. J. van Parys, Ph.D., Director of Worship, with the Basilica's bell, called the tintinabulum, and umbrellino. The umbrellino was made for the Basilica by Phyllis Lehmberg.

Right: Director of Social Outreach, Janice Anderson.

Director of Worship Johan van Parys feels a direct connection between the liturgy and the outreach programs at the Basilica.

"The liturgy is really the heart of this community. But if the liturgy stays within the church building, it's nothing but meaningless ritual turns. The liturgy needs to propel people out. A few years ago, when Mother Teresa died, a local television station went out and asked people what does this mean to you? They went under the bridge right here by the Basilica, where homeless people live. And they asked the people there, 'Who is Mother Teresa to you?' And their answer was, 'It's Janice Anderson and the Basilica of Saint Mary.' Janice Anderson is our director of Social Outreach. That is the best comment I could have ever hoped for about worship at the Basilica."

Community life can include romance, too, as in the story of William and Danette King.

"I believe the second time I went to Mass, Danette was the reader. After seeing her read that morning and a couple of other times, I began to think that I would like to get to know her better. After all, she had a beautiful voice, she was pretty, she looked like a nice person, and her faith was important enough to her to go to daily Mass.

"I'm a little shy and was unable to get up the nerve to talk to her. Then, on Valentine's Day 1997, she came in to Mass late, during the Gospel. It was fairly crowded and one of the only available seats was next to me and she took it. After Mass, as I was fumbling with my coat trying to think of what to say to her, she began to talk to me. We struck up a conversation and talked for a few minutes. As we were leaving, I figured, 'What the heck' and asked her if she would like to have coffee with me sometime. The first date went great except that when we got to Starbuck's we realized neither of us drank coffee.

"We began to see each other regularly and our relationship grew a lot at the Basilica because we saw each other there every morning. We used to stand outside by the rectory and talk before we left for work. The regulars at morning Mass watched as our relationship developed.

"Later, we were married in the Basilica. Many of our friends from the 7:00 A.M. Mass were there and served as our eucharistic ministers. We asked Father Martin Fleming, who normally said the 7:00 A.M. Mass on Tuesday, to preside."

BASILICA

MAGAZINE OF THE BASILICA OF SAINT MARY · IN RECOGNITION · SPRING 1996

Making an Impact —
Young Adults at the Basilica

Right: In 1993, a group of young parishioners from the communications industries redesigned the parish bulletin. Then they decided to do a newsletter. And as the story goes, they got a week or so into that idea when somebody said, "Well, heck, let's do a magazine instead." Now the glossy and beautiful Basilica Magazine, *produced entirely by volunteers—even the printing is donated—has a circulation of nine thousand both within and outside the parish, telling the story of the Basilica and its people in stories and columns accompanied by professional photography.*

Right: The Chiron School operated in the old Basilica School building during the nineties.

Far right: In September of 1996, the Basilica's Committee to Promote Justice organized its first project in cooperation with Habitat for Humanity.

Left: Father Joseph Gillespie broke ground for the new entry into the undercroft.

Right: Families gathered in the undercroft before construction began.

Development of the undercroft—the very large Basilica basement—
is designed to create space to serve the poor and to provide meeting
rooms and much-needed bathroom space. McGough Construction's
Gordy Anderson likes the friendly atmosphere and the challenge.
"There is no comparison to working on an office building. With the
Basilica, often there just isn't any documentation. If plans ever
existed, they have been lost. Everything is a challenge. You have no
idea what you'll get into."

THINKING ABOUT THE FUTURE

*T*here is only one way into a vibrant future, and that is through the committed effort of people who have made the Basilica of Saint Mary an ongoing part of their lives. Talking about the history and place of the church, people at the Basilica are energetic, even buoyant. But when you are part of a landmark, even conversations about the past tend to slip toward the future. The Basilica parishioners know that looking back also means looking forward into an accelerating new century.

In the year 2000, the mission of the Basilica of Saint Mary is defined this way. "The Basilica of Saint Mary is a community rooted in the gospel of Jesus Christ. As the Co-Cathedral of the Archdiocese of St. Paul and Minneapolis it is our mandate to model, to inspire and to provide quality liturgy, faith formation, pastoral care, and hospitality; preach justice and provide emergency relief to the poor; pursue interfaith relationships; contribute to the celebration of sacred arts in this community. The parish is marked by hospitality and a rich diversity of age, ethnic, racial, social, and economic backgrounds."

This last is an intentional aspect of the Basilica's work and purpose. Father Michael O'Connell has given it considerable thought.

"Diversity is difficult to characterize but I can tell you that people constantly say that they feel comfortable immediately when they walk in the door. Young adults, single people for example, feel very comfortable here. They might feel odd in a typical suburban parish with so many married couples with children. An older single person doesn't feel so odd here either,

because there are so many different kinds of people readily visible to the eye. Somebody recently divorced or separated, especially a woman, feels very comfortable here. It's the same thing for a gay or lesbian person, or a person of color. When you come in, you're right away going to know that you're not the only one like you."

Part of the Basilica's growth during the nineties results from the welcome and hospitality it has extended to other populations that are coming to the Twin Cities. There is, for example, a new influx of Liberians into the parish. Father O'Connell points out that Liberia is not the only source of our present immigrants.

"Minneapolis in the late nineties has been the recipient of a great number of west and east African peoples. There is civil war in a number of the countries that run along the west African Coast. There are a lot of political refugees and a lot of them have found their way to Minneapolis, and to the Basilica. They felt welcomed here, and then we began to try to listen to their stories, support them here, and in some cases help their families out and over here."

Director of Worship Johan van Parys adds: "Our understanding of church has become much more global; its very essence is diverse. If we really want this community to be diverse, and be an image of the larger church, then we have to pay attention so that people find somebody who looks like them. And if we are not intentional about it, it will not happen. People need to find a saint who looks like them in their church. People need to find music that sounds like them in their church. Church and worship are for the entire community."

Many people, it appears, can find some aspect of the Basilica to involve their minds, energies, and souls. Joanne Provo thinks that "the building draws them in, the liturgy really engages their senses, and then I think it's those outreach programs, those activities—education, women's spirituality, whatever they're looking for—that really engages them soul-deep."

Parishioner Carolyn Baldus says frankly, "I think this parish really speaks to my soul. When I go in there, I just feel like I'm surrounded by these enormous arms of God. As much as I need to eat food every day, the Basilica really nourishes my soul."

Once engaged, people tend to become involved. "We volunteer not for personal glory, not to see our names in headline type, but because we want to make a meaningful contribution, we want to make this community, this world, a better place," says parishioner Margaret Nelson. "This place," says Dr. Kim Kasling, "does have some kind of nonquantifiable charisma for community. I go all over the country, Canada, and Europe—very, very few have this feel."

In eleven months of 1999, six hundred and fifty comments were recorded in the Basilica visitor book. All fifty states were represented, plus Wales, New Zealand, the Philippines, Australia, Paraguay, Israel, The Netherlands, Germany, Argentina, Venezuela, Guam, England, Ireland, Mexico, Kosovo, France, Italy, Switzerland, South Africa, Malta, Slovakia, Japan, Puerto Rico, and Canada.

Many people's comments centered on the beauty and serenity of the building, surrounded now, as it has been for years, by scaffolding and workers' trucks. It is clearly a work in progress, as trustee Joanne Provo knows.

"While working on the undercroft renovation, it finally dawned on me that this church, like all grand cathedrals, like all such spaces, will never be done. In fact, they really shouldn't be done. It's almost selfish for us, now, to want to do it all, because it doesn't engage the next generation, and the next and the next. I have finally realized that this building is going to outlast all of us. Every single generation, every single group that comes here needs to own a piece of the restoration and renovation. They have to. The programs and the people that are within it will change and even the building will continue to change. But

what will stay is what it represents. What will stay is the beacon that it represents for the city."

Father O'Connell is fond of quoting Jeremiah 29:7: "Seek the well-being of the city to which I have sent you; pray for it to the Lord. For in its well-being, you shall find your own."

Each act inside the community of the Basilica of Saint Mary, whether serving a sandwich, writing a check, joining a choir, or just opening up and singing in the congregation on Sunday morning, carries the work of the parish into the uncharted territory of the future. Through its complex and resilient web of faith and activities, places like the Basilica of Saint Mary help people stay together, well-guided, as we move forward.

Father Martin Fleming, who has been involved at the Basilica of Saint Mary for nearly fifty years, says, "There's a song that makes me think about the Basilica. 'All are welcome, all are welcome, all are welcome in this house.' "

"All are welcome, all are welcome, all are welcome in this house."

SOURCES

Reardon, James Michael. *The Basilica of Saint Mary of Minneapolis: Historical and Descriptive Sketch.* St. Paul: The North Central Publishing Co., 1932, 1955.
—. *The Catholic Church in the Diocese of St. Paul: Earliest Origin to Continental Achievement.* St. Paul: The North Central Publishing Co., 1952.

1994 Minneapolis Fast Facts. Minneapolis: Municipal Information Library, 1994.
Population Abstract of the United States, 1993 ed. McLean, Va.: Documents Index, Inc., 1993.
Timetables of History. New York: Simon and Schuster, 1982.
The Value of a Dollar 1860-1999, 2nd ed. Lakeville, Ct.: Grey House Publishing, 1999.
Annual household income figures from *The Value of a Dollar* that appear in the chapter timelines are averages derived from standard jobs in all industries for the given year.

The Basilica of Saint Mary Archives contain the author's manuscript, with source notations, and the author's research files. The files hold a collection of parishioner memoirs, church papers and documents, and copies of the photos and graphic materials. The archives also hold complete transcriptions of the author's interviews, and a set of audiotapes of the interviews themselves.

PHOTO AND ILLUSTRATION SOURCES

Photographs and other illustrations pictured in this book appear courtesy of the institutions, collections, or persons listed below.

MHS: Minnesota Historical Society
ASPM: Archdiocese of St. Paul and Minneapolis
BSM: Basilica of Saint Mary Archives
CB: *Catholic Bulletin*
BM: *Basilica Magazine*
Reardon: *The Basilica of Saint Mary of Minneapolis: Historical and Descriptive Sketch*

COVER: ASPM
Back cover: Michael Jensen
Half title: *Catholic Bulletin*
Frontispiece: MHS

INTRODUCTION: x, all MHS collection; 2 clockwise, Burg collection, Klein collection, Piazza collection, De Lisi collection; 4 clockwise, BSM, Morony collection, Gulden collection, De Lisi Glenn collection, Piazza collection; 6 clockwise, Piazza collection, De Lisi Glenn collection, Scheinost collection, BSM.

BEFORE THE BASILICA: 8 MHS; 9 CB; 10 Piazza collection; 11t Reardon, 11b Reardon; 12l Gulden collection, 12r MHS; 13l ASPM, 13r CB.

BUILDING THE BASILICA: 14 ASPM, 14inset BSM; 15t BSM, 15b MHS; 16 BSM; 17l Michael Jensen, 17r Michael Jensen; 18 Pirner collection; 19l Gooley collection, 19r BSM; 20l Keith collection, 20r Keith collection; 21l CB, 21r BSM.

THE EARLY YEARS: 22 Ostlund collection; 24 BSM; 25 ASPM; 26t Hennepin History Museum, 26b Reardon; 27l Michael Jensen, 27r CB.

THE TWENTIES: 28 BSM; 29 BSM; 30 BSM; 31 BSM; 32 CB; 34l Neubauer collection, 34r Michael Jensen; 35l Connors collection, 35r BSM; 36 Piazza collection; 37 BSM; 39 Minneapolis Public Library; 40t BSM, 40b CB; 41 BSM.

THE THIRTIES: 42 BSM; 43 BSM; 44 MHS; 45 BSM; 46t BSM, 46b Michael Jensen; 47 BSM; 48t Zuccaro collection, 48b Zuccaro collection, 48r Zuccaro collection; 49l Michael Jensen, 49r Michael Jensen; 50 BSM; 51 Hennepin History Museum.

THE FORTIES: 52 BSM; 54 BSM; 55 Michael Jensen; 56l Michael Jensen, 56r BSM; 57l Piazza collection, 57m Piazza collection, 57r Michael Jensen; 58 MHS; 59 BSM; 60l Miner collection; 60r Michael Jensen; 61 Piazza collection.

THE FIFTIES: 62 Capecchi collection; 64 Burg collection; 65 Michael Jensen; 66l Piazza collection, 66r BSM; 67 ASPM; 68 *The Diapason*; 69 BSM.

THE SIXTIES: 70 Hennepin History Museum; 72 Berg collection; 73 BSM; 74l BSM, 74r MHS; 75 Berg collection; 76 University of St. Thomas; 77l Michael Jensen, 77r BSM; 78 BSM; 79 all Korb collection; 81 Hennepin History Museum.

THE SEVENTIES: 82l Cunningham collection, 82t BSM, 82b BSM; 83t Gulden collection, 83b BSM; 84 BSM; 85l Pirner collection, 85r BSM; 86l Gulden collection, 86R Kuklock collection; 87L Munnich collection, 87r Michael Jensen; 88 Munnich collection; 89l Christensen collection, 89r Michael Jensen; 90 Pirner collection; 91 Michael Jensen.

THE EIGHTIES: 92 BSM; 94l BSM, 94r unknown; 95 University of St. Thomas; 96 Babcock collection; 97l BSM, 97r Hunstiger collection; 98 CB; 99l BSM, 99r Hunstiger collection; 100 Michael Jensen; 101 CB.

THE NINETIES: 102 *Minneapolis Star Tribune*; 103 Losinski Hettinger collection; 104 Friends of the Basilica and Mary Dunn Brown; 105 Michael Jensen; 106 Michael Jensen; 109l BSM, 109r Gulden collection; 110 Michael Jensen; 111l *Minneapolis Star Tribune*, 111t BSM, 111b Hunstiger collection; 112 unknown; 113l Michael Jensen, 113r Nelson collection; 114 Michael Jensen; 115l Michael Jensen, 115r unknown; 116 Michael Jensen; 117l Michael Jensen, 117r Michael Jensen; 118l Michael Jensen, 118r Rau-Barber; 119l Michael Jensen, 119r Michael Jensen; 120l, 120r Diana Gulden; 121l *Catholic Spirit*, 121r O'Connell collection; 122l Michael Jensen, 122r Michael Jensen; 123 Michael Jensen; 124l Kluckholhn collection, 124r Michael Jensen; 125l Michael Jensen, 125r Diana Gulden.

THINKING ABOUT THE FUTURE: 126l Michael Jensen, 126t Janel Lewandowski, 126b Rau-Barber; 127t unknown, 127b Michael Jensen; 128 clockwise Ann Durn, Michael Jensen, Michael Jensen, Michael Jensen; 130 clockwise Michael Jensen, Peter Beck, unknown, *Minneapolis Star Tribune*; 131t Michael Jensen, 131b Peter Beck; 132 *St. Paul Pioneer Press*.